Priceless Computer Tips at Your Fingertips

By

Sudhir Diddee

Copyright and Disclaimer

Send comments to book@vyanjan.com

ISBN-13: 978-1466395923

ISBN-10: 1466395923

Library of Congress Control Number: 2011918009

i

To my Parents,

in-laws and

Dr. Pandey:

Thank you for the values and wisdom which keep me grounded.

And to Seema, for your love and support

Acknowledgements

This book represents the very "tip of the iceberg" effort of thousands of engineers and product managers of various products listed within this book. These extremely talented and passionate groups, who have thought long and hard on various aspects of our everyday computing and productivity needs, make it easier for all of us. This book stands on the shoulders of those giants.

I have been fortunate to work in a great company and have been influenced by Microsoft Co-founder Bill Gates and Microsoft CEO Steve Ballmer on what it is to think BIG. In fact, my brother-in-law gave me a book by Mr. Gates which was the catalyst for my current job.

I learned a great deal about product management and business from the blogs of Microsoft leader Steven Sinofsky. Two managers immensely influenced my career: Ken Park and Amir Khan. Ken taught me to pursue my passion. I will forever be indebted to him as he is the paragon of a great manager. Amir was a great mentor who could delicately balance eastern and western management styles.

I would like to thank my editor Jim Flack, designer Stephanie Brachat, Peggy Li, Kim Spilker and Rosemary Caperton. Finally, there are the wonderful colleagues, too many to list here, with whom I am fortunate to work and learn from every day, and who make my company truly the best place to work.

Extended family plays a big role in a typical Indian life and mine is no different. My family's role in my life is indelible.

Finally, I need to thank my wife Seema for her unwavering support, my kids Abhinav and Ananya for being extremely patient as I worked to write the book on weekends last summer and through the Christmas holidays. My son even suggested a title: "Save time to spend more time with your kids." I realize now writing a book and finding publishers is extremely hard, but I promise to make up for the all the lost time.

Table of Contents

Intended Audience

This book is intended for the average office worker. In my experience, most modern-day office workers are familiar with some features of commonly used software. However, either due to lack of time or being creatures of habit, it is difficult to discover new ways of doing things. And who has the time to read the manual? We are go-getters who like to figure things out ourselves. Though in hindsight, I wish I had read a few manuals before starting a few projects!

Some users will find some of the tips straight-forward and basic. For those who know them and for those who don't know, they realize they should have been using it all along. However, I can assure you that even the "Power Users" of the products mentioned in this book will learn something new!

How to use this book

As with everything in life, changing old habits is hard. The same is true for benefiting from the tips in this book. Various research scholars on human behavior have suggested that it takes 21 days to form a habit. I think that is a good benchmark. The best way to use this book is to take any one section at a time and practice the tips till they become second nature.

You should review the section on **The Windows Graphical User Interface** in the Appendix to familiarize yourself with the elements of a program window, to make the most of these tips. Take a printout of the Cheat Sheets at the end of the book and pin them next to your computer at work and home. Every time you want to save time using one of the tips, check yourself if you fall back to doing it the old way. Soon you will be addicted to the new method.

Finally, the best way to learn is to teach others. There is no substitute for the sheer pleasure and satisfaction of enabling a colleague, friend or a new user to learn a more efficient way to work, and you get to practice one more time. Remember to be curious. There is a community of passionate users out there willing to teach and learn. This work itself stands on the shoulders of giants since I learned these over the years through friends, colleagues, websites and sheer curiosity. If you come across a valuable tip, please feel free to e-mail me at: book@vyanjan.com

I hope you have as much fun using this book as I had writing it.

The Middle Seat

I wanted to give a little bit of background on how the idea for this book came about. I was traveling from Houston to Miami and had a middle seat. My co-passengers were an adorable old couple going to visit their daughter and grandkids in Florida. I offered to exchange my seats with either of them so that they could be together, but it turned out they wanted the seats that way! Both of them wanted the window seat, and the one who lost got the aisle seat. So I was stuck with the middle seat and I took out my laptop and started working.

The lady asked what I did for a living, and I mentioned I worked at Microsoft. The lady peered over my shoulder and asked about the benefit of Microsoft Windows 7. She had just gotten a new laptop as a gift from her daughter and she did not see the benefit of all the new Microsoft Windows 7 features people were talking about. I asked her where she worked before she retired, and she mentioned she was a school teacher. Armed with a bit of her background I told her to give me five minutes of her time so that I could show her some of the programs.

I proceeded to demonstrate some of the new cool features of Microsoft Windows 7, Microsoft Outlook 2010, and Microsoft Excel 2010. Before we realized it, almost 45 minutes had passed, and she was still engrossed. She suddenly stopped and was nodding her head. I asked her what happened and she said:

"I just wish I had known these tips sooner. It would have saved me so much time! **Why don't you write a book on this, so that I can have a ready reference when I need it?"**

Later that night in the hotel room, I was up till 3 a.m. thinking about her comments, and I began sketching the idea on my notebook until I had an outline and the core of the book laid out. A few months after that chance meeting, the book was finished.

This book is designed for beginners to advanced users, and hopefully even power users will find a few tips which are new to them. I wanted to write the book in a format that cuts to the chase and gets users up and running. The idea is that a user who spends two hours with this book should learn a lot of new tricks and can begin reaping productivity gains right away.

Also these are *my favorite tips,* but they are in no particular order. Most of these programs have hundreds or thousands of features and each of these has taken several hundred hours of design, development and testing before it is integrated into the product. No one could ever possibly capture all these features in a single book.

I also hope my dad finishes this book, because he is an example of the power of these products that empower users worldwide. He is 100% self-taught and has learned to use computers in retirement. I hope after he reads this, we will spend more time talking about something besides troubleshooting the latest feature he discovered that week. Daddy, the Problem Steps Recorder application that you will learn about in this book is exactly for users like you!

Microsoft Windows® 7

These tips can be used with Microsoft Windows 7. Many of these tips will use the Microsoft Windows Logo key found on most modern keyboards. It is usually to the left of the spacebar (which is the longest key on the keyboard) and next to the keys labeled **ALT** and **CTRL**. In some laptops the Windows Logo key is in the top row towards the right.

The Microsoft Windows Logo key has this symbol on it:

Figure 1

In all the tips where I mention the **Microsoft Windows Logo key**, please refer to this key.

1. Locking your machine

Let us start with security first. The first rule of security is to never leave your machine unlocked. To quickly lock your machine, hold the **Windows Logo key + the "L" key.**

2. Taskbar

If you are working on a Microsoft Word document or a Microsoft PowerPoint slide deck, and you need to start a new document or slide deck, you can do so right from the application's icon on your task bar.

- **Shift + Left click** on the icon starts a new instance of the application (such as a new document or slide deck), even if the application is already running.

If you have multiple instances of a program (e.g. multiple documents or multiple PowerPoint presentations) open and want to cycle through them quickly, use the following command:

- **Ctrl + Left click** on the icon will cycle between the open documents in that application

3. Jump list

Jump List is one of the best features of Microsoft Windows 7. It's designed to provide you with quick access to the documents and tasks associated with your applications. For example, right-clicking on the Microsoft Outlook icon in your taskbar gives you a few common Outlook options:

- Compose a New E-mail Message
- Set up a New Appointment
- Create a New Contact
- Create a New Task

Figure 2

Right-clicking on the Microsoft Excel icon shows you a list of your recently used workbooks, or the chance to launch a new workbook.

If you are a developer and you write applications on the Microsoft Windows platform, please use the Jump List feature to light up your applications and make them infinitely more useful for your end users. They will thank you for it every day.

4. Quick Desktop Search

The Desktop Search feature has completely changed the way I work on my machine. I no longer need to be diligent on how I file my content, since anything on my machine that has the term I am looking for is brought instantaneously to the screen. So, if I type in a phrase that was referred to in an e-mail thread, that email comes up. If I am looking for a feature in Windows but don't know where to navigate in the control panel, I just type in the name of the feature in the Search box. If you are looking for an article you e-mailed a friend, it will find the article, the e-mail, and any references to it on your machine.

Here is where you will find the Search box:

Step 1 - Go to **Start,** which is the Windows logo in the far lower-left corner of your screen

Figure 3

Step 2 - Click on **Start** to reveal the menu

Step 3 - Simply start typing in the box called *Start Search, located* under **All Programs**

Figure 4

If you start using this specific feature, you will notice a perceptible change in productivity and reduced time for desktop search queries.

Another way to bring up the Search option is to use the Microsoft **Windows Logo key + the "F" key** to find any file.

5. Snipping Tool

This has been one of my most-used features though not enough users know about it. Similar to the Insert Screenshot or Microsoft OneNote screenshot(see tip 69 or tip 91), this feature takes a snapshot of any image you choose on your screen and allows you to paste it into a document or email, or to edit and save the image for your use.

Steps to follow:

Step 1 – While on the screen you want to snip, click on the **Snipping Tool** icon

Figure 5

If you haven't yet used it, you won't see the Snipping Tool icon on the Windows Ribbon. Just type "Snipping Tool" in the Search box, as shown below and hit the **Enter key.**

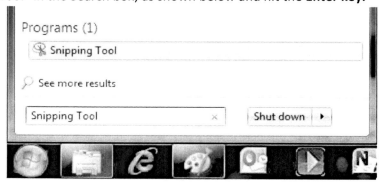

Figure 6

Step 2 - Select the section of the screen you want to snip

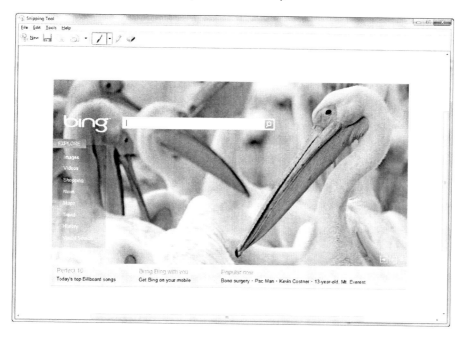

Figure 7

Step 3 - You can then use **Ctrl + the "C" key** to copy that snip, go to your chosen document, and use **Ctrl + "V" key** to paste the snip into that document. You can also choose one of the options to **"Save As"** or **"Send To"**. You can also highlight or annotate sections of the image.

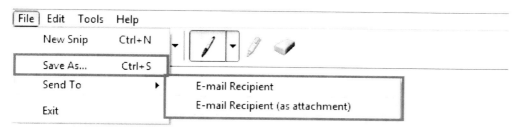

Figure 8

6. Aero Shake

If you need to cut through a cluttered desktop to focus on a single window, **Left click** on the title bar of any window. While holding the mouse button, give your mouse a shake. Every open window, except for the one you've selected, will minimize. Shake again, and they all come back.

In the example below, I am working on an Excel workbook, and want to close all other documents/windows. I will **Left click** on the Title bar next to "Book1- Microsoft Excel," and give it a shake.

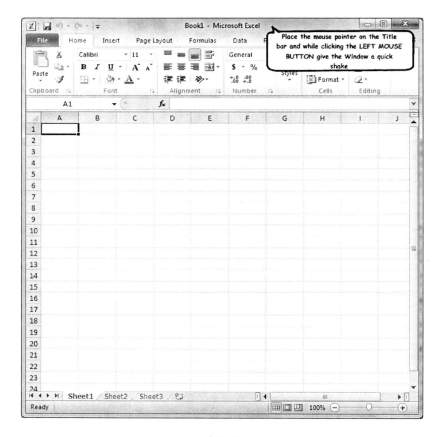

Figure 9

7. Show Desktop

If you have several windows open, to quickly view your desktop, hold the **Windows Logo key** + the "D" key.

 Another way is to go to the lower right corner of your screen (to the right of the date and time display) and mouse over the rectangular box.

Figure 10

8. Split Window - Windows Snap

Anyone who has worked on budgeting or analyzing reports and has had to contend with collating information across two programs into the *final* deck or document can identify with the nightmare it can be. Comparing printouts or cutting and pasting the numbers across the programs can be a tough task. This single improvement has saved countless hours for me. Here's how it works:

For a quick way of resizing windows, use Windows Snap. Simply drag a window to the edge of your screen and it will expand vertically taking up half of your screen. Do it again for your second document, for side-by-side comparisons. Snap makes reading, organizing, and comparing documents easy.

For example, say you have a Microsoft PowerPoint document and a Microsoft Excel spreadsheet. Click on the mouse and drag the Microsoft Excel spreadsheet to the farthest right of the screen, until you see a vertical rectangle.

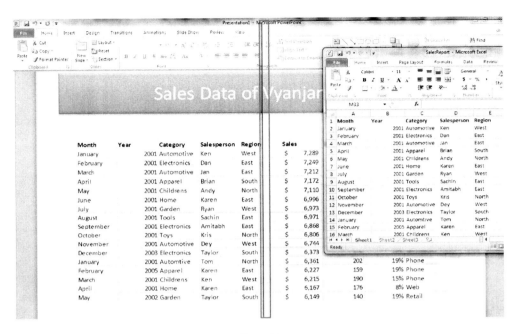

Figure 11

Move the Microsoft PowerPoint document to the farthest left of the screen, and you will see the two windows side by side.

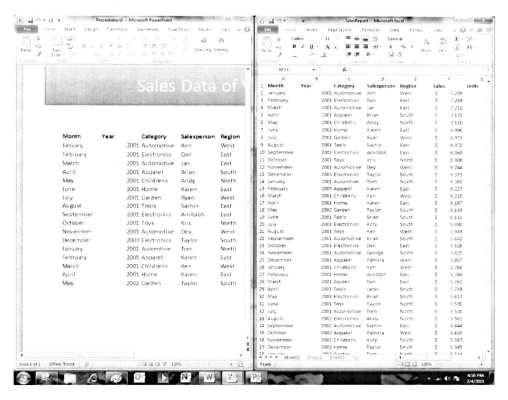

Figure 12

Shortcuts to move the screens left and right:

Windows Logo key + Left Arrow key	Maximize the window to the left side of the screen.
Windows Logo key + Right Arrow key	Maximize the window to the right side of the screen.

The next two tips apply to laptops.

9. Connect to a Projector

Among several productivity features included in Microsoft Windows 7, this one has to rank at the top. Countless minutes have been lost in conference rooms around the world as people try to figure out which combination of keys to use to project the presentation onto the screen. With Windows 7, that is no longer a problem. Just hit the **Windows Logo key + the "P" key** and you are given four options. Choose the option that suits you, and you are ready to go. It is also handy when you are working on dual monitors.

Windows Logo key + P - To connect to a second monitor or a projector

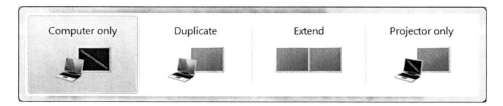

Figure 13

10. Access the Mobility Center

To quickly get to the mobility center, hit the **Windows Logo key + the "X" key**

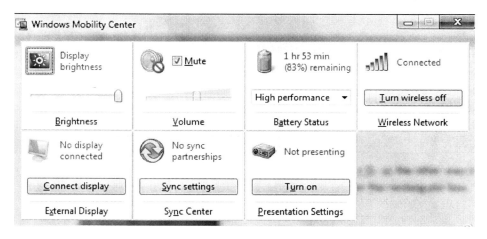

Figure 14

11. Quick Launch

Quick launch is one of the biggest time savers introduced in Microsoft Windows 7. Though you might have seen taskbar shortcuts in various iterations of Microsoft Windows, it has never been easier. Let's say you have an application that is internal to your company which you use several times a day, or perhaps your role requires you to use a program like Microsoft Paint many times in the day, but it is not a part of the Microsoft Windows 7 ribbon interface. You can quickly add the application in three simple steps. Look at the standard taskbar at the very bottom of your screen:

Figure 15

Now I want to add Windows Live Messenger or another program installed on my machine to my taskbar. I navigate to the application by going to **Start, All Programs** and find the application.

Here are the steps:

Step 1: Locate the application on your machine by clicking on the Microsoft Windows **Start** button.

Figure 16

Step 2: Right-click in the white space next to the application name and select **Pin to taskbar**

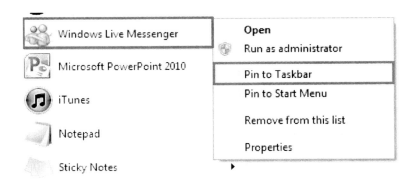

Figure 17

Step 3: The application Quick Launch button is added to your taskbar

Figure 18

Another way to achieve the same result is to **Pin the program to taskbar** when the program is running. Right-click on the taskbar and left click **Pin this program to taskbar.** Similarly, if you wish to unpin the program so that it is no longer on your taskbar, **right click** it when it is running and choose **Unpin.**

Figure 19

12. Sticky Notes

Almost all office workers identify with "sticky notes" around their work place. One of the cool features of Microsoft Windows 7 is **Sticky Notes**.

Go to Start and type in "Sticky Notes"

Figure 20

Programs (1)

Sticky Notes

Figure 21

Click on the program and you will see a sticky note appear on your computer desktop; you can start typing on it.

Figure 22

Right Click the mouse while the cursor is on a note to change the color of your note. You can click the **+ icon** in the upper left corner of the note to add another note. Click the X in the upper right corner of a note to delete it. Click a note and press **Alt + F4** to close the note windows; all notes are automatically saved.

13. Additional Clocks

One of the advantages of a distributed workforce is the ability to tap into the unlimited talent pool which is spread out geographically. However, managing time zones can be challenge. But you can add additional clocks, reflecting your most commonly used time zones.

Click on the clock at the bottom of the screen:

Figure 23

And click on "**Change date and time settings.**"

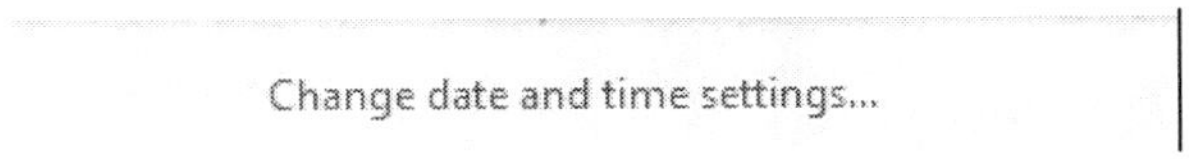

Figure 24

Or, use the search box to type "**additional clocks**"

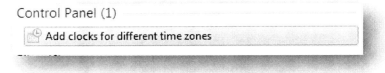

Figure 25

Control Panel (1)

Add clocks for different time zones

Figure 26

You may select the clocks you want to add:

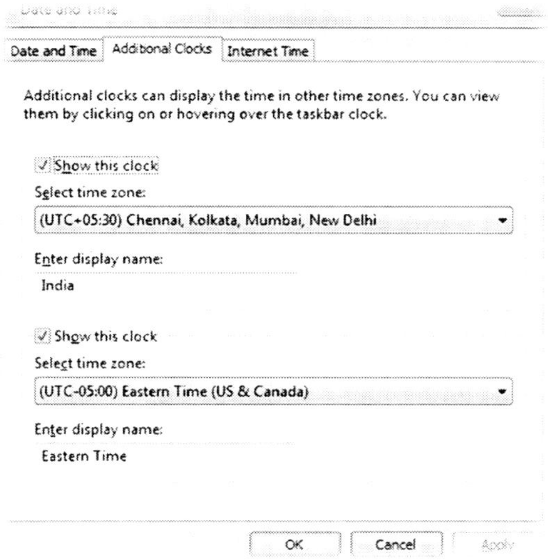

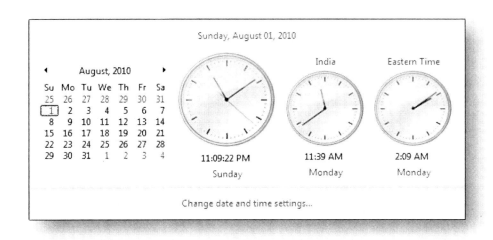

Figure 27

When you click on lowest right corner of the Task Bar, you will see the clocks:

Figure 28

14. Problem Steps Recorder

Have you ever been able to recreate an issue, but unable to describe it to your help desk? The Problem Steps Recorder tool is a simple screen-capture utility that takes screenshots of every click of the keyboard and move of the mouse. Turn it on to record this data into a zipped report page that can be e-mailed directly to someone who can help, such as a friend or help desk support representative.

Troubleshooting errors for a remote user can be very difficult since you cannot actually see what's happening. The new Problem Steps Recorder allows someone to see exactly what's happening, recording every action that takes place on the remote machine.

Every step of the user's actions is logged, complete with a screenshot with the item highlighted, and it even allows you to provide commentary on specific details.

To launch the Problem Steps Recorder, follow these steps:

Step 1 - Click Start and type **Problem Record** in the search bar
Step 2 - Select **Record** steps
Step 3 - Click **Start Record**, and then proceed through the steps to recreate the problem. You can use the Comment feature to note anything specific to a screenshot
Step 4 - Click **Stop Record** when you have the information
Step 5 - In the **Save as** dialog box that appears, type a file name, then click **Save**. The file will be saved with a .zip file extension, which you can then e-mail to the person helping you.

This is also an excellent tool for **training document generation**, such as teaching colleagues a new tool, or for when someone is leaving a team and wants to create handover documents.

15. Change Desktop Background

Many people like to have wall paper on their Desktop, usually a favorite picture or image. If you want to change the desktop background, Microsoft Windows 7 makes it easy:

Step 1 – View your Microsoft Windows 7 Desktop

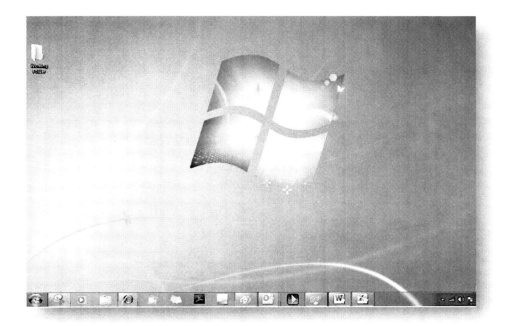

Figure 29

Step 2 - Right-click anywhere in the Desktop background and click on **Personalize**

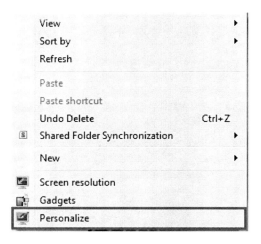

Figure 30

Step 3 - Select one of the Aero Themes ("Landscapes") or click on **Get more themes online** to see a collection of breathtaking images from Bing.

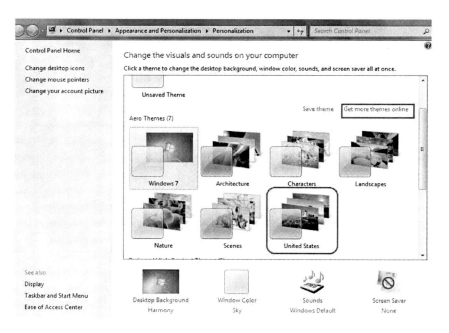

Figure 31

And you are done! The desktop changes to a new background.

Figure 32

To change it to a new image, select **Next desktop background** and the next image of the collection appears. Or "shuffle" images to have a new desktop image every few hours.

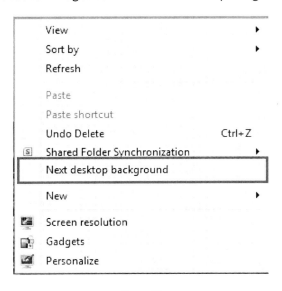

Figure 33

16. Libraries

Libraries are a new concept introduced in Microsoft Windows 7. They make it easier to manage information and files scattered across a computer or home/work network. Libraries are like a collection folder, without having to move the files.

Here's an example: you are doing a "road show" to five cities. You have a video, trip report, photos and a slide deck to present to customers in each city.

One way to organize this information is to have five folders, one for each city, each with its videos, photos, slides, and documents. Another way would be to have all videos in one folder, all pictures in another folder, and so on.

Normally this would mean duplication, but with Libraries, you can have a folder for each city which would hold the information for videos, documents and pictures, and you can quickly sort and shuffle them. My entire home collection of home videos and pictures uses libraries extensively, because they are scattered across several computers and external hard drives.

You can learn more about Libraries at *http://windows.microsoft.com/en-US/windows7/products/features/libraries*

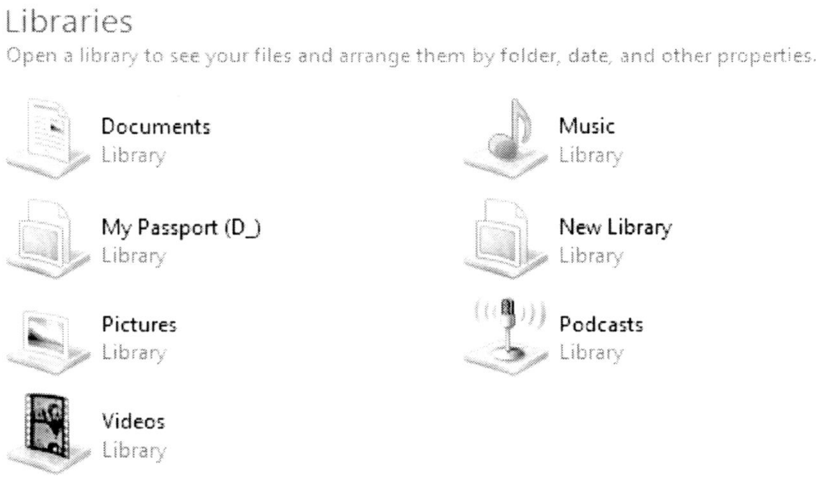

Libraries
Open a library to see your files and arrange them by folder, date, and other properties.

Documents
Library

Music
Library

My Passport (D_)
Library

New Library
Library

Pictures
Library

Podcasts
Library

Videos
Library

Figure 34

Microsoft Outlook® 2010

Microsoft Outlook is business and personal e-mail management software used by more than 500 million users worldwide. Most information workers use it to manage their e-mail and calendars. With the following tips you will begin to scratch the surface of what is possible. Hopefully you will begin your own journey of self-discovery of tools specific to your own productivity needs.

17. Create a New E-mail Message

Let's begin with a simple task: creating a new e-mail message in Microsoft Outlook. If you are like a typical user, you create anywhere between 10 to 25 new e-mails a day, in addition to responding to others.

To quickly create a new e-mail message, just click **CTRL+N**

18. Quickly Send a Message

To send an e-mail message, click **CTRL + Enter**

Especially for those who send multiple e-mails in a day, the precious seconds saved from just these two tips will soon add up.

19. Rules

One of the biggest problems people face is e-mail overload. However, most of the e-mail can be easily managed by setting rules where e-mails from certain people or teams can go directly into a particular folder. For example, e-mails from your manager can be routed into a separate folder. E-mails sent to you where you are in the "cc line" can go to a different folder, or your e-mail stock alerts can go to your investing folder.

Here are the steps to create rules:

Step 1 - Click on **Rules** under the Home Tab

Figure 35

Step 2 - Click on the e-mail for which you want to create a new rule and click on **Create Rule**

(In this case we are creating a rule for MarketWatch© Alerts.)

Figure 36

Step 3 – You will see the rule conditions

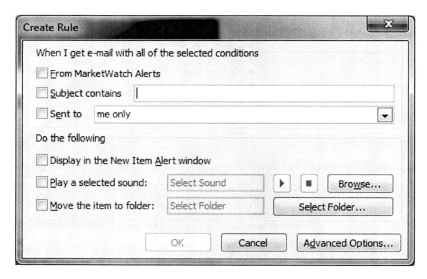

Figure 37

Step 4 - Select the conditions for the **Move to MarketWatch Folder** rule

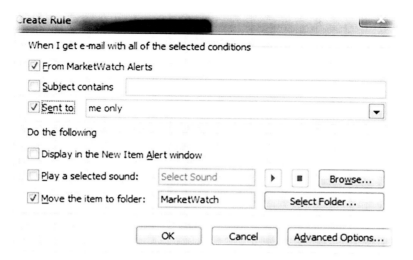

Figure 38

20. Recall a Sent Message

Have you ever experienced that sinking feeling after hitting "Send" on an email that would have benefitted from one more review? In the event that you send an e-mail too soon without reviewing it completely, you can "recall" it. Here's how:

Step 1 - While in Microsoft Outlook, open the message in your Sent Items box that you wish to recall or resend

Step 2 - Click **File** in the top left corner, above the **Ribbon**

Figure 39

Step 3 - Look at the Info for the message, and go to the **Message Resend and Recall** section

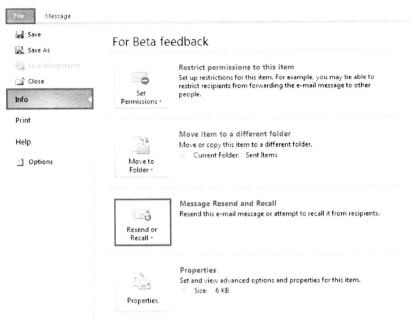

Figure 40

Step 4 - Click the **Resend or Recall** button

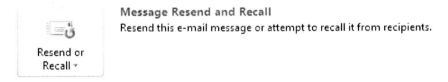

Figure 41

Step 5 - Select **Recall This Message**

Figure 42

Step 6 - You will be prompted with a dialog box for options for the recall.

You can:

- Delete unread copies of the message or
- Delete unread copies and replace with a new message.
- Check the box labeled "Tell me if recall succeeds or fails for each recipient" if you wish to be informed.

Figure 43

Step 7 - Click **OK**

21. Voting Buttons

If you want to quickly poll your team members on available options, such as the kind of food to order for a team meeting, the voting button meets this need:

Step 1 - Start a new e-mail message
Step 2 - Click on **Options** and select **Use Voting Buttons**

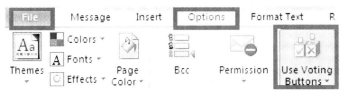

Figure 44

Step 3 - Click on the **Arrow** and Select **Custom**

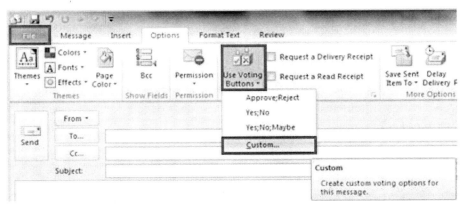

Figure 45

Step 4 - Enter the voting options – in this case the kind of food to order. Make sure the options are separated by semicolon (;)

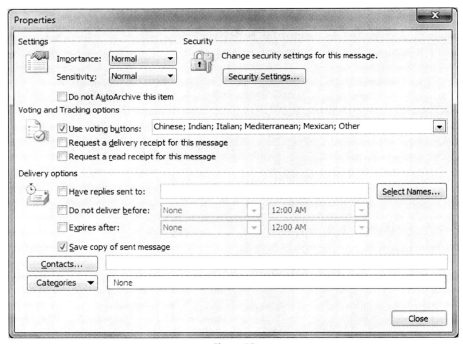

Figure 46

Step 5 - Click on **Close**

Step 6 - When the users receive the e-mail, they can make their choice by clicking on the Vote button

Figure 47

Step 7 - The respondents can make a selection from the **Vote** icon

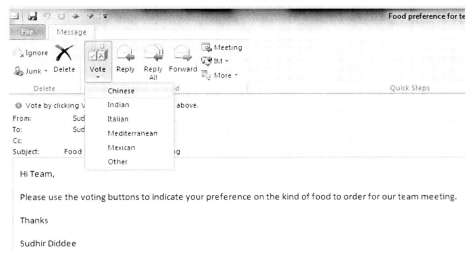

Figure 48

Step 8 - The e-mail responses show the user preference

Figure 49

22. Automatically Close the Message After Replying or Forwarding

If you are an office worker, you will invariably end up having 8 to 10 e-mails open, and after a while, you end up closing all of them. This can be really annoying and wastes a lot of time. One way to overcome this is to configure your Outlook options to close your e-mail after you have replied or forwarded.

Step 1 - Open **Microsoft Outlook**
Step 2 - Go to the top of the **Ribbon** and click **File**

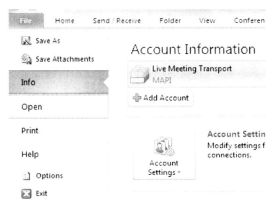

Figure 50

Step 3 - Click on the **Options** button

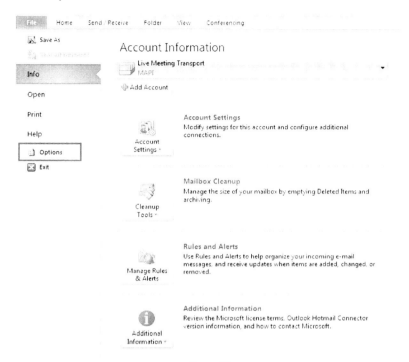

Figure 51

Step 4 - In the left pane, select **Mail**

Step 5 - In the right pane, scroll down to the **Replies and forwards** section

Step 6 - Click the "Close original message window when replying or forwarding" checkbox. **Click OK**

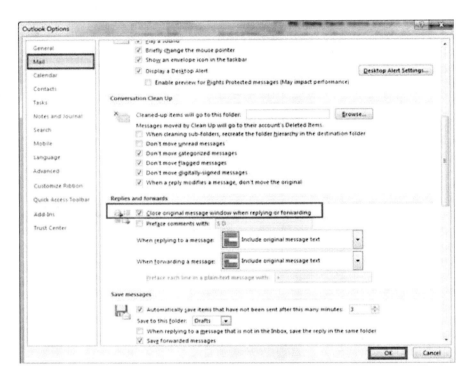

Figure 52

23. "Direct Replies To"

If you are sending a message that requires a response that other people must also receive, use the **"Direct Replies To"** feature. This ensures that when each recipient clicks on reply, all of the applicable addresses will automatically be in the "To" field, eliminating both the reliance on the recipient to remember to select "Reply all" and the extra time you may need to spend on forwarding the replies.

Step 1 - On a new e-mail message, click on **Direct Replies To**

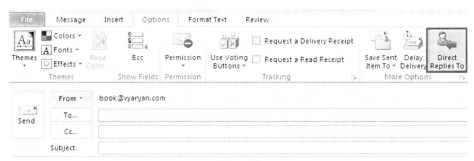

Figure 53

Step 2 - Check the box **Have replies sent to** under Delivery options

Figure 54

24. Permanently Delete an E-mail Message

To permanently delete a message, just hit **Shift + Delete**. This comes in especially handy when you are trying to delete an e-mail that is huge in size, and you don't want it in your Deleted Items folder.

25. Resolve Name Typed in an Address Field

To quickly resolve an alias name in an e-mail address field (To, cc, bcc), type in **CTRL + K.**

Automatically Resolve Address

Putting an "=" in front of the e-mail alias that you are trying to resolve when composing a mail will automatically resolve it to any exact matches.

What is an email alias? An email alias is an abbreviated email address that points to your real email address. It could also a forwarding email address that points to your real email address. E.g. support@vyanjan.com could go to sudhir@vyanjan.com

26. Quick Steps

Quick Steps are a life-saver if you want to file e-mail or need to send e-mails to the same group. Quick Steps evolve as you go through various projects to suit specific needs.

Some Quick Steps are created automatically for you by Microsoft Outlook, and you can also create some to meet your needs. I have one for Order Confirmation for all my online purchases. I also have one for tracking all summer camp information for my kids. At the end of the summer, I might delete the Summer Camp Quick Step and replace it with School Work or something else.

Let's say I am planning a vacation to Turkey. There will be a lot of planning from research, tips from friends, tickets and hotels. In order to track everything, I create a folder called Vacation Turkey. I want to put all my pertinent e-mail into this folder so that I can file it away as I plan and track my trip.

Here are the steps to create a Quick Step.

Step 1 - Locate Quick Steps under the Microsoft Outlook Ribbon and select **Create New**

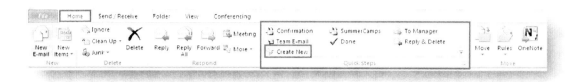

Figure 55

Step 2 - Select **Move to Folder** and Change Status to **Mark as Read**

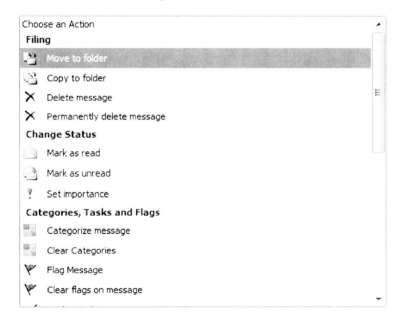

Figure 56

Step 3 - Choose the Folder

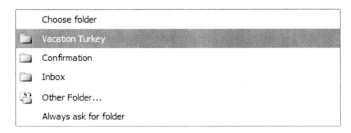

Figure 57

Step 4 – Select **Finish** under Edit Quick Step

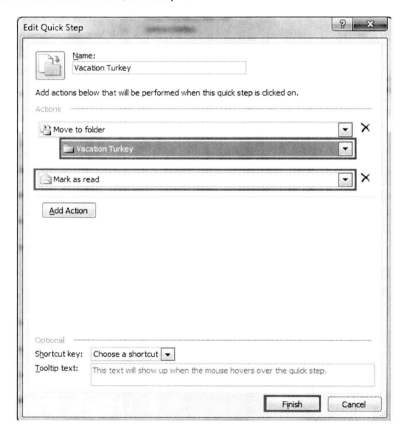

Figure 58

There are some smart scenarios built into the default Microsoft Outlook, and the Microsoft Outlook team has done an excellent job on this. Some of the common prebuilt Quick Step scenarios are:

- **Meeting Reply** – Some conversations on e-mail can get too long or may only be solved by scheduling a meeting. Just click on Meeting Reply and all the people on the thread get automatically added to the meeting.
- **To Manager** – If you need to send an e-mail to your manager, this Quick Step is useful.
- **Team E-mail** –If you need to distribute some information to your team, Team E-mail Quick Steps comes in handy.
- **Team Meeting** – Useful for setting meetings with a team or group.

There are two steps to go to a Quick Step folder. You can hold down the Control key while clicking on the Quick Step to navigate to the folder

Figure 59

Or right-click on any Quick Step which has an associated Move Step to navigate to that folder

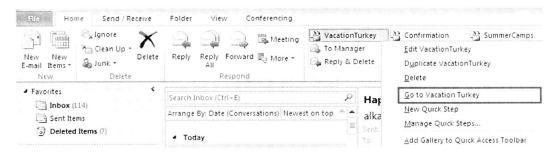

Figure 60

27. Out of Office

(Note: The out-of-office assistant only shows up if you are using a Microsoft Exchange server. If you don't have an Exchange server, you can emulate the same process using Rules -see Tip 19.)

For most users of Microsoft Outlook, this feature is not new; however, it can be used as a productivity tool too. For example, if you are involved in a project and do not want to be disturbed, you can set the Out of Office message as "Busy with critical projects, will respond to all e-mails tomorrow." This sets expectations and can be really effective.

One cool feature in Microsoft Office 2010 is to set different Out of Office messages for internal and external customers. For example, you can list your cell phone for your team members when you head out on vacation, while pointing external customers to a team e-mail address or other appropriate direction.

If you have never set an Out of Office message, here are the steps for Microsoft Office 2010:

Step 1 – Go to **File**, **Info**

Figure 61

Step 2- Select **Automatic Replies** (Out of Office)

 Automatic Replies (Out of Office)Use automatic replies to notify others that you are out of office, on vacation or not available to respond to e-mail messages.

Figure 62

You can set the following options:

- Select a specific time period

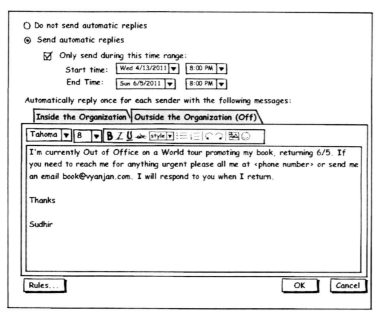

Figure 63

Use the "Inside" and "Outside the Organization" tabs to tailor your message.

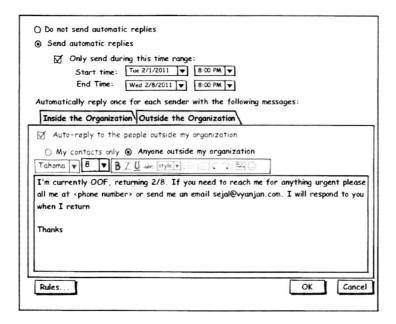

Figure 64

For people outside the company, you have the option of sending these responses to only your contacts or to everyone.

Step 3 - Click OK

Step 4 - The Automatic Replies (Out of Office) will notify you that Automatic Replies are being sent.

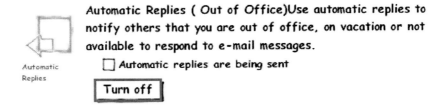

Automatic Replies (Out of Office) Use automatic replies to notify others that you are out of office, on vacation or not available to respond to e-mail messages.

☐ Automatic replies are being sent

Turn off

Figure 65

You can click Turn Off to stop sending automatic replies, or they will automatically cease if you entered an End Time when setting up the notification.

Turn Off

Figure 66

28. Instant Search and Features

If you are using Microsoft Outlook Instant Search often, just type in **CTRL+E** to quickly get to the Instant Search box.

As the e-mail load increases for information workers, more and more information is stored in Microsoft Outlook and it has become the default document repository. Search E-mail has become a life saver, but here are some tricks which will take this feature to a whole new level.

This is a simple search example where I search for "Marketwatch." All the e-mails with the term "Marketwatch" are returned, with the search term highlighted.

Figure 67

The senders are MarketWatch Bulletin, MarketWatch e-Newsletter, and MarketWatch Alerts. The number of items is listed in a status bar. In this case we have 151 items and these results are not very useful.

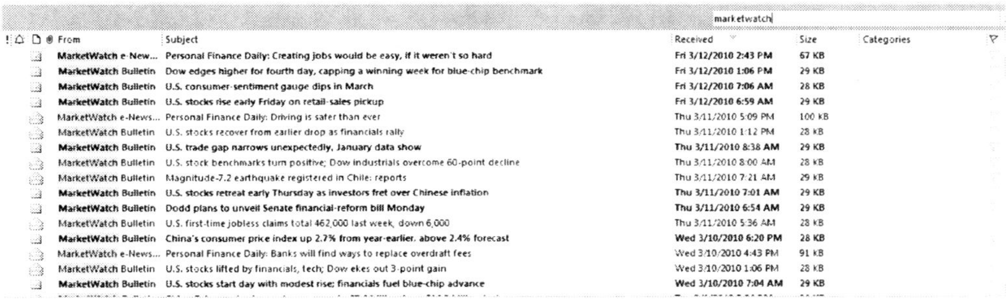

Figure 68

Let's say you were searching for an e-mail that you recall was sent by MarketWatch Bulletin, and had a subject line which mentioned consumer sentiment. There are steps to quickly get to the e-mail. Enter the following in the Search Box, and watch your lost email magically appear:

From: MarketWatch Bulletin **Subject:** consumer

Figure 69

Or, let's assume someone sent you an e-mail with a Microsoft PowerPoint attachment. You can quickly get to that e-mail by typing the following string:

From: Person's Name **Attach:*.pptx**

Example: From: Sailesh Attach:*pptx ; From: Sujaya Attach:*.docx

It will return all e-mails from that person with a Microsoft PowerPoint attachment (or other file types).

You can also use: **hasattachments: yes**

Figure 70

You can configure the search options by going to **File, Options, Search.** You can define the Scope, refine search criteria like From, Subject, Categorized, Importance etc.

29. Advanced Find

Advanced Find is really for finding that very elusive message. Bring up Advanced Find by pressing **CTRL + SHIFT + F.** You have a lot of options you can use in the three tabs of the box, but a combination of a few criteria leads to desired results.

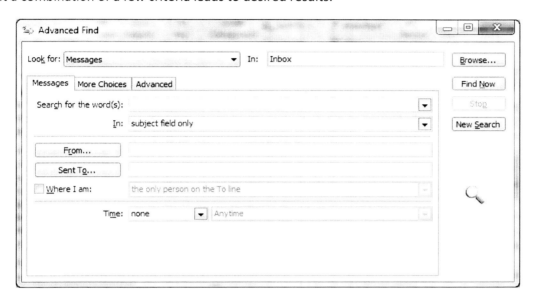

Figure 71

In this example, I am trying to find a Marketwatch e-mail by entering any specifics that I recall

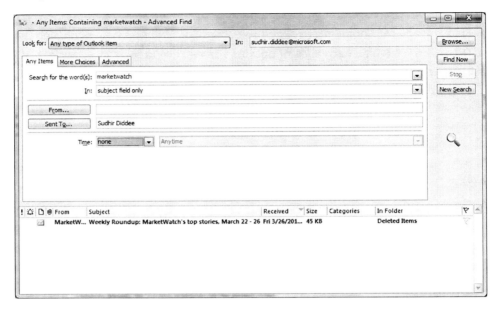

Figure 72

You can set custom options for the highlight color or search speed, etc.

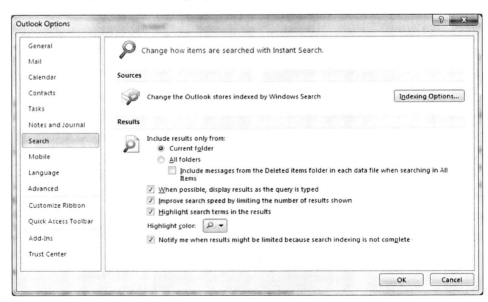

Figure 73

30. Signature

If you run a small business or are in a big company it is always a good idea to include a signature with your contact information at the end of your e-mail. You can create a unique signature for each of your e-mail accounts or choose between different signatures for a single account. To create a signature, follow these steps.

Step 1 – Go to **File, Options**

Figure 74

Step 2 – Go to **Mail, Signatures**

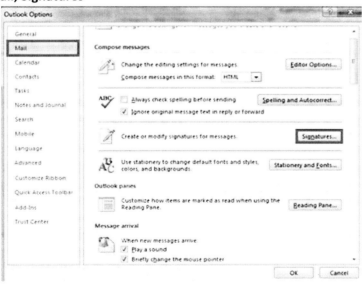

Figure 75

Step 3 – Select the **E-Mail account** and **click New**

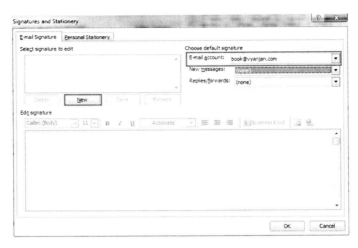

Figure 76

Step 4 – Give a name to the signature

Figure 77

Step 5 – Type in the Signature in **Edit Signature** section and **click OK**

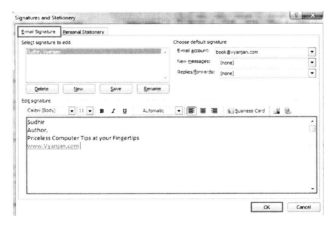

Figure 78

Step 6 – **Click OK** as shown in the figure below

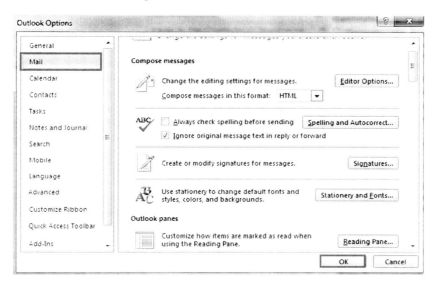

Figure 79

Next time you create a new e-mail, your signature will appear automatically as shown below:

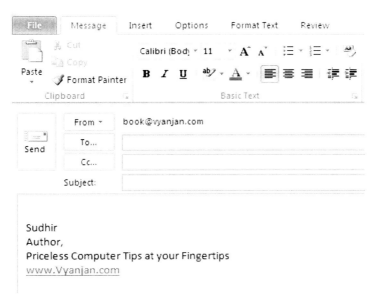

Figure 80

31. Views

Views are one of the best features of Microsoft Outlook 2010. You can have preconfigured views if you quickly want to see certain filters.

Figure 81

For example, some people want to start the day with just unread e-mail.

Click on **Change View** to select

- Views which show only high importance **(!)**
- View of e-mails from your manager
- A weekend view where only certain messages are filtered through
- By categories, etc. You can create custom views based on your unique needs.

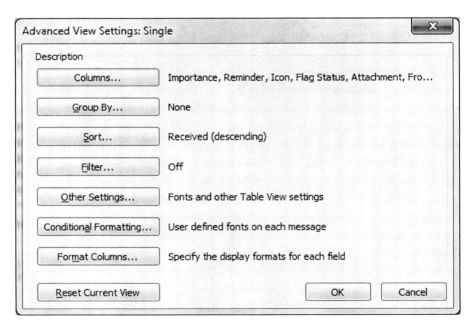

Figure 82

32. Clean Up

If you click on the Clean Up button, it will move all the old and redundant messages in your conversation to the Deleted Items folder.

Figure 83

- Clean Up always keeps the most recent message around, ensuring you have all the content in the conversation while allowing you to delete the redundant messages.
- Clean Up is intuitive enough to keep messages that have attachments, flags or categories.
- Clean Up is available on an individual conversation or a whole folder, and can be customized to move the redundant content to any folder in your store.

33. Ignore

This is one of the best features of Microsoft Outlook 2010. It does require Microsoft Exchange Server 2010, but is very useful if you find yourself on an e-mail thread you don't want to be on. Let's say you were added to your office's sports fantasy league. This is not your personal passion, and the number of e-mails is overwhelming. Just click the **Ignore button** while on any e-mail of that thread. The Ignore button quickly and easily moves an entire conversation -- *and* any future items that arrive -- to your Deleted Items folder.

Figure 84

34. Conversation View

One of the common complaints of users is to find an inbox full of messages, several of which relate to the same conversation. If you switch on the **Conversation View**, all your e-mails are grouped into conversations based on the subject of the e-mail. This is especially helpful on your first morning back from a two-week vacation. To turn on the **Conversation View**, here are the steps to follow:

Step 1 - Go to **View** and Check the box **Show as Conversations**

Figure 85

Step 2 - Select the appropriate folder when prompted

Figure 86

Step 3 - All of your e-mails appear as conversations

If you expand a conversation, you can see all related messages, including your replies from your Sent Items. The software is so slick that it even tracks who replied to someone else. You should definitely try it; it is likely you will get an immediate productivity boost in your e-mail handling.

35. Quick Parts

Quick Parts is a lifesaver if you constantly find yourself typing the same text over and over again. You may know that you can set up signatures to quickly insert into an email (see Tip 30). Quick Parts is like a signature that you can insert anywhere in an e-mail. For example, say you are often asked for directions to your office. Instead of cutting and pasting (or worse, retyping) all the time, you can type in "Here is the address", hit the **Enter key**, and the auto-text that you have set up will insert the directions. Other ideas for use of Quick Parts are inserting a list of

50

resources you frequently need to send to people you work with on projects, internal and external site references, etc. Quick Parts can save you a lot of time.

Here are the steps:

Step 1 - Create a new e-mail message
Step 2 - Type in the text that you want to use as a **Quick Part**
Step 3 - Highlight the text and select **Quick Parts** from the Text tab of the **Insert** ribbon

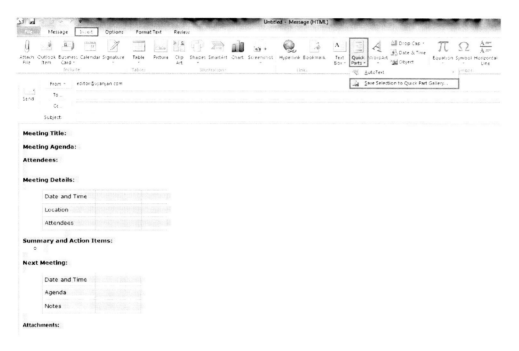

Figure 87

Step 4 - Click on **Save Selection to Quick Part Gallery**

Step 5 - Give it a name and enter the **Category** and **Options**. And you're done!

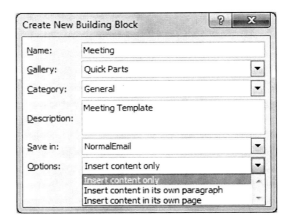

Figure 88

Next time you create a document, just type in the name of the Quick Part and it will appear where the cursor is blinking. Hit **Enter**.

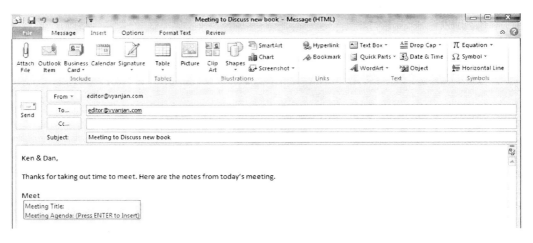

Figure 89

Here is how it appears

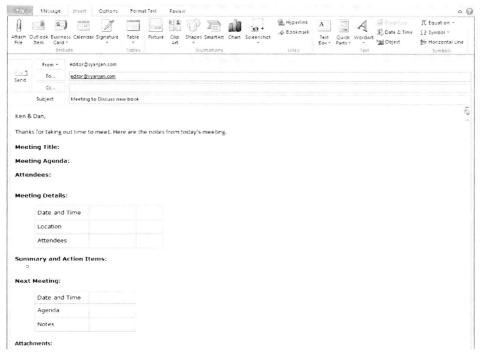

Figure 90

36. Organize by Colors

It can help you save time to visually sort your mailbox by using colors. E.g. to make your manager's e-mails to you pop, have them appear in red text. E-mails which are sent only to you can appear in blue text. E-mails sent to a group you belong to, e.g. Weekend Cyclists, can appear in purple, and so on.

To customize and view your e-mail by color in Microsoft Outlook 2010 here the steps:

If your inbox looks like this:

▲ Date: Yesterday					
	Dale Carnegie Training	Sudhir Diddee	Daily Dose of Confidence	Tue 9/7/2010 6:13 AM	24 KB
▲ Date: Monday					
	Dale Carnegie Training	Sudhir Diddee	Daily Dose of Confidence	Mon 9/6/2010 6:08 AM	23 KB
▲ Date: Last Week					
	Dale Carnegie Training	Sudhir Diddee	Daily Dose of Confidence	Fri 9/3/2010 6:05 AM	23 KB
	Dale Carnegie Training	Sudhir Diddee	Daily Dose of Confidence	Thu 9/2/2010 6:06 AM	23 KB
	Dale Carnegie Training	Sudhir Diddee	You're Invited to Attend How to Sell Like a Pro	Wed 9/1/2010 9:50 AM	33 KB
	Dale Carnegie Training	Sudhir Diddee	Daily Dose of Confidence	Wed 9/1/2010 6:07 AM	23 KB
	Dale Carnegie Training	Sudhir Diddee	Daily Dose of Confidence	Tue 8/31/2010 6:13 AM	23 KB
	Dale Carnegie Training	Sudhir Diddee	Daily Dose of Confidence	Mon 8/30/2010 6:07 AM	23 KB
▲ Date: Two Weeks Ago					
	Dale Carnegie Training	Sudhir Diddee	Daily Dose of Confidence	Fri 8/27/2010 6:06 AM	23 KB
	Dale Carnegie Training	Sudhir Diddee	Engaging Ideas: Stand out with Effective Presentation Skills	Thu 8/26/2010 10:47 AM	35 KB
	Dale Carnegie Training	Sudhir Diddee	Daily Dose of Confidence	Thu 8/26/2010 6:07 AM	23 KB
	Dale Carnegie Training	Sudhir Diddee	Daily Dose of Confidence	Wed 8/25/2010 6:05 AM	23 KB
	Dale Carnegie Training	Sudhir Diddee	Daily Dose of Confidence	Tue 8/24/2010 6:12 AM	23 KB
	Dale Carnegie Training	Sudhir Diddee	Daily Dose of Confidence	Mon 8/23/2010 6:06 AM	23 KB

Figure 91

And you want your inspirational e-mails from the mailing list "Daily Dose of Confidence" to appear in Green, here are the steps:

Step 1 - Click on View

Figure 92

Step 2 - Click on **View Settings**

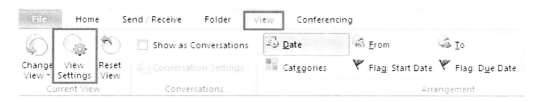

Figure 93

Step 3 - Click on **Conditional Formatting**

Advanced View Settings: Compact

Description

Columns...	Header Status, Importance, Icon, Attachment, From, To, S...
Group By...	None
Sort...	Received (descending)
Filter...	Off
Other Settings...	Fonts and other Table View settings
Conditional Formatting...	User defined fonts on each message
Format Columns...	Specify the display formats for each field

Reset Current View   OK   Cancel

Figure 94

Step 4 - Click on **Add**

Figure 95

Step 5 - Click on **Condition**

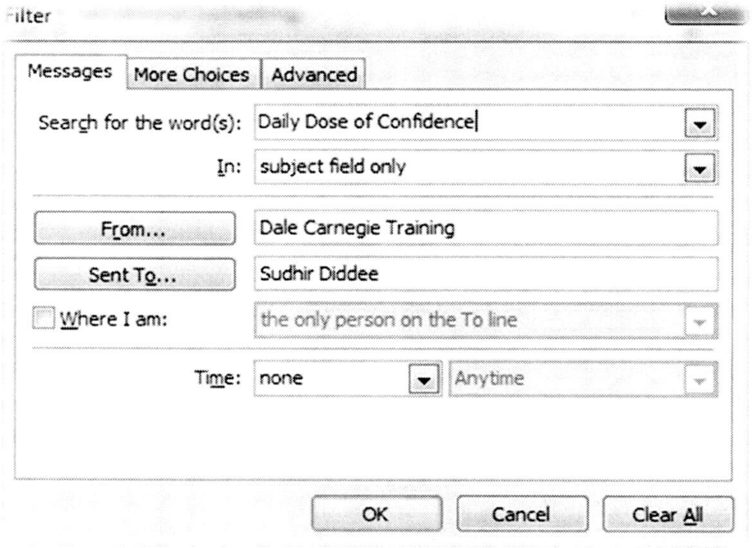

Figure 96

Step 6- Click on **Font,** assign a unique font and color and click **OK**

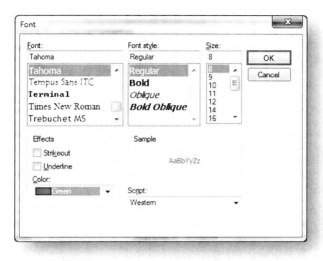

Figure 97

Step 7 - Click **OK** and exit the window

Figure 98

Step 8 - Your e-mail view will change. My Daily Dose of Confidence e-mails will now appear in GREEN

Figure 99

37. E-mail Template in Microsoft Outlook

Let's say you have a standard template for monthly reports, meeting minutes or for project management status updates. Instead of creating a new e-mail and copying from a Microsoft Word document, you can use e-mail templates. You would create your template once, and from then on you can modify the relevant sections.

Here is how it works:

Step 1 - Create a new e-mail message
Step 2 - Enter e-mail addresses of regular recipients

Step 3 - Enter the text, in this case the "Meeting Minutes" template

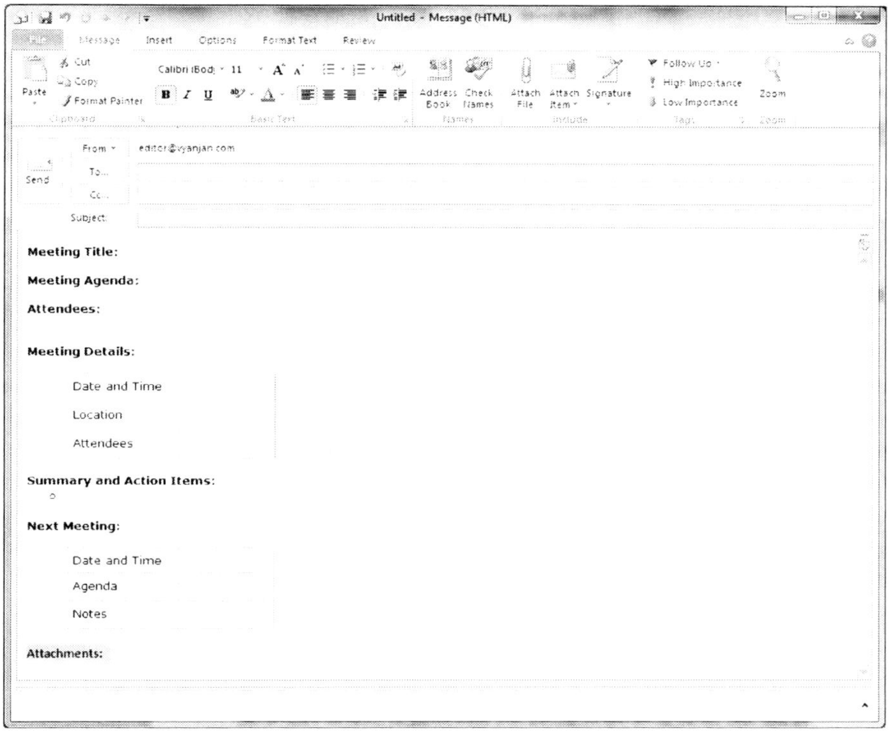

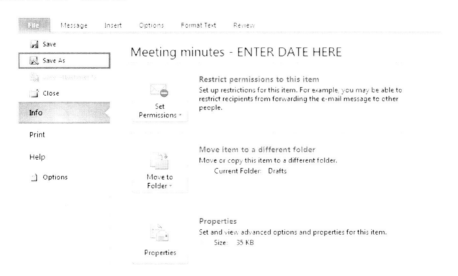

Figure 100

Step 4 - Click on **File – Save As**

Figure 101

Step 5 - In the drop down menu, select **Outlook Template**

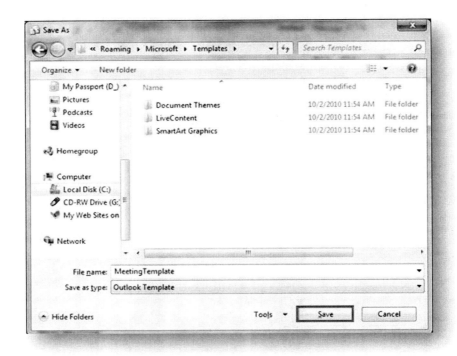

Figure 102

Step 6 - Give the name to the template, and click **Save**

Your template is saved in this directory by default:

C:\Users\USER NAME\AppData\Roaming\Microsoft\Templates

You can change the directory structure to any directory you want.

To create a new e-mail using your template, follow these steps:

Step 1 - Click **File**, **Open**
Step 2 - Browse to the template directory (or to where you saved your template)
Step 3 - Open the template, change anything you need to change and you're all set

38. Insert Screenshot within an Outlook message

Say you are working on a project or researching a product online. You might come across an image or information that you want to share with a friend or colleague. One way to share the image is to use the Snipping tool to e-mail the image (See Tip # 5). However, it might be just as efficient to insert the screenshot within Outlook. Here is how it works.

Let us say you see the website shown below, and you get an idea that you want to run by your team.

Figure 103

To send it as a Screenshot within Outlook, follow these steps:

61

Step 1 – Click on **File, Insert, Screenshot**

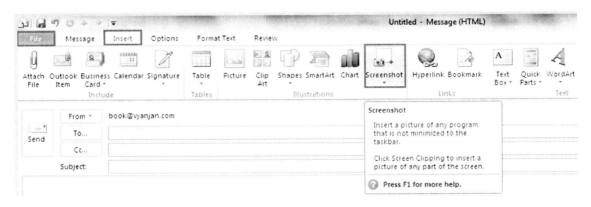

Figure 104

Step 2 – You will see all Active windows. Mouse over to select the window you want and **Left click.**

Figure 105

Step 3 – The whole screenshot is inserted in the body of the email.

Figure 106

Step 4 – This is optional: you can work with the formatting tool to crop the image, and only keep the section you want in the body of the email. The formatting tool bar is shown below:

Figure 107

And here is an example of an edited section of the screenshot:

Figure 108

Only one screenshot at a time can be added. To add multiple screenshots, repeat steps 1 and 2.

39.Tasks

One of the most productive ways to use Microsoft Outlook is to use the Tasks tab. In fact, everything you do can be managed as a Task.

- You can create a Task by clicking New Task, or by pressing **CTRL+SHIFT+K.**
- You can assign new Tasks to someone else and track them.

Tasks are also a way for you to keep a track of completed jobs if you need to quickly see what you accomplished in a given time period. You can also drag an e-mail to Tasks and create a new Task, by right clicking:

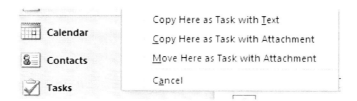

Figure 109

You can move an e-mail to the Task as an attachment. This is very useful if you have several e-mails which contribute to the task at hand, so that you have all the information and attachments needed to complete the Task in one place. Obviously, Tasks can be a whole topic in itself.

40. Create Tasks Quickly

Tasks are a great way to plan your workday and if you start planning your work around tasks vs. email you will notice a distinct improvement in your personal productivity.

If you want to quickly create a new Task, press **CTRL+SHIFT+K**. A new Task window will open.

41. Calendar: Create a Meeting Start Time by Clicking in the Free Space

In your Calendar view, if you want to set a meeting at 2:00, just double-click on any hour marker or the open space at 2:00 to open a calendar entry. Not every calendar entry has to be a meeting. You can use your calendar as a "tickler file" by adding recurring tasks, such as "this month's newsletter article due," and set it to recur every four weeks. By marking this entry as **free time**, it won't take up a meeting slot and entries marked as "free time" aren't visible to team members setting up meeting times on your calendar.

Figure 110

42. Microsoft Outlook Meeting Request

One of the cool features of Microsoft Outlook 2010 is the Microsoft Outlook meeting request. The request shows where this meeting would fall on your calendar, along with any meetings you may have next to it. So, when you get a new meeting request from someone, you can quickly see any adjacent meetings, so you can respond accordingly. This is very useful if you haven't blocked your calendar for a commute or an offsite visit.

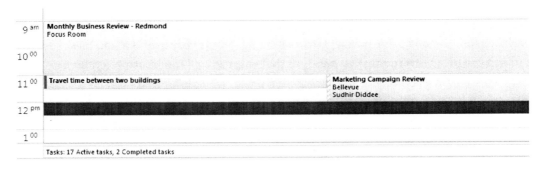

Figure 111

43. RSS Feeds into Microsoft Outlook

Linking RSS feeds from any blog or website into Microsoft Outlook is an easy three-step process.

Step 1 - Right-click on the RSS feeds folder in Microsoft Outlook and click on **Add a New RSS Feed**

Figure 112

Step 2 - Add the location of the RSS feed you want to enter

Figure 113

(Example: http://blogs.technet.com/technet_flash_feed/rss.xml)

Step 3 - Click on **Add** and you're done

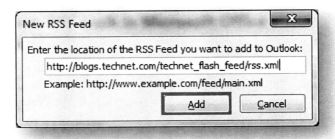

Figure 114

Microsoft Excel® 2010

Microsoft Excel is the business world's preferred number-crunching program. It can be used to perform tasks from basic math calculations to advanced scientific spreadsheets, with an amazing array of functions and formulas built in to help you. With the built-in charting tools and data pivot capabilities, you have at your fingertips one of the best software programs ever built.

44. Creating a Formula

This is a well-known trick for anyone who knows Microsoft Excel well. And for the rest of us, it is immensely helpful. I dedicate this tip to a good friend who is nothing short of a genius in his field of computer science. I call him Raja (which stands for king in India) of coding. My friend can literally dissect any operating system or any piece of software in a matter of hours. But, one day I saw him struggling with something and asked why was he hesitant in using Microsoft Excel for what he was trying to accomplish. He told me point blank (as only friends can) that he did not know Microsoft Excel well enough, since he didn't use it in his day-to-day work. This was probably the only time I felt we were peers in terms of level of intelligence.

For all the folks who have never written a formula in Microsoft Excel, it is easier than you think, and more helpful than you can imagine. Here is how it works:

Let's say you have three labeled columns: one is "Item," the second is "unit price," and the third is "quantity." You want to calculate the total for each row. Looking at the figure below, go to the Total column for Paint, and simply type in B2 X C2 in cell D2, preceded by an "=" sign, and you're done. The "="sign indicates to Excel that the following is a formula.

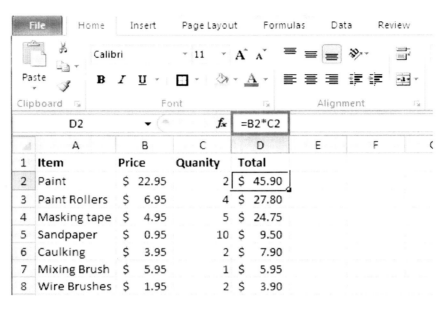

Figure 115

The standard mathematical operators will apply, and Microsoft Excel uses the symbols "*" for multiplication, "/" for division, "+" for addition, and "−"for subtraction.

These formulas in Excel are so powerful that many financial and business professionals make their living crunching Excel spreadsheets filled with very complex multi-level formulae. But even knowing only the most basic types of formulas will keep your budget or inventory spreadsheets singing. And when you later have to update one part of the spreadsheet, everything downstream of that change will automatically update.

You will find Microsoft Excel functions in the following categories:

  Database functions
  Date and time functions
  Engineering functions
  Financial functions
  Information functions
  Logical functions
  Lookup and reference functions
  Math and trigonometry functions
  Statistical functions
  Text functions

45. View All Formulae at Once

When working on projects, we might often get a spreadsheet or workbook to review that has been programmed by a colleague. To view all the formulas on the spreadsheet just enter **CTRL and "~"** (the tilde symbol).

Here's an example

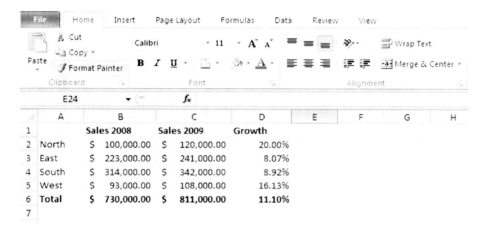

Figure 116

To see the formula view, hit **CTL + "~"** within the spreadsheet. To go back, hit **CTRL+ "~"** again.

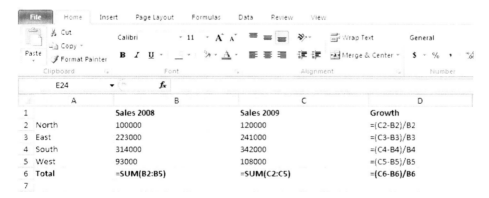

Figure 117

46. Conditional Formatting

Let's assume you have a lot of data and you quickly want to see some values visually. The best tool to do this is conditional formatting. In regards to the table above, if you want to know the most expensive items vs. least expensive, you can do the following:

Step 1 - Select the column
Step 2 - Click on **Conditional Formatting** on the **Home** tab

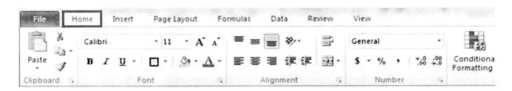

Figure 118

Step 3 - Click on the down arrow and make a selection

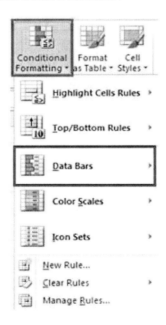

Figure 119

In the example below, I selected **Data Bars**

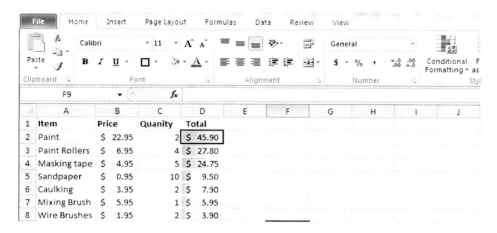

Figure 120

If you select **Icon Sets**, the view changes to

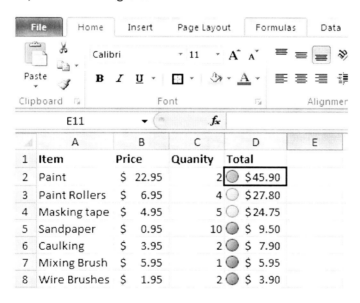

Figure 121

Now you can quickly see the items less than $10.

47. Day Calculator

When working on various projects, you may need to know how many days there are between two given dates, so that you can allocate resources accordingly. Even though Microsoft Project is the perfect solution for any project planning work, for most users Microsoft Excel has some really cool functions built in.

Networkdays: You can enter two dates in cells say B1 and C1. Enter the following in cell D1

=Networkddays(B1,C1). In the below example, we will have 22 weekdays.

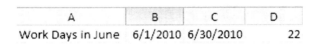

A	B	C	D
Work Days in June	6/1/2010	6/30/2010	22

Figure 122

Weekday

To know the day of the week for 6/1 in the preceding figure, , instead of looking at the calendar, just type in:
=weekday (cell number with the date in it) (in this case: "=weekday (B1)"
This example is to calculate the value of cell B1 type in the value as shown below:

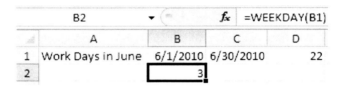

B2			f_x	=WEEKDAY(B1)
	A	B	C	D
1	Work Days in June	6/1/2010	6/30/2010	22
2		3		

Figure 123

The answer is 3, which means 6/1 falls on a Tuesday. Sunday is treated as the first day of the week and Saturday the last, and so this goes 1 through 7.

48. Pivot Tables

Pivot tables are, without a doubt, my favorite feature of Microsoft Excel. Even though they have been around for nearly 15 years, people may not know about them. Once they know, they love them. But what is the big deal about Pivot tables?

Let's say you have some sales data for your company that you want to analyze:

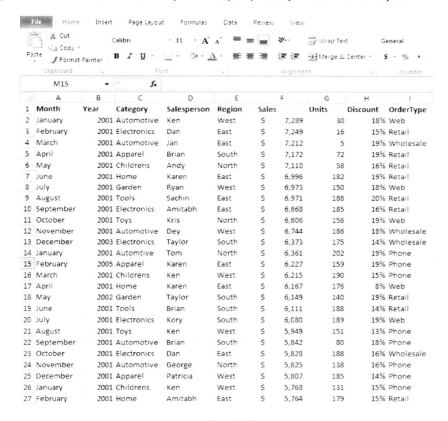

Figure 124

Now let's say you receive three simple questions from your manager:

- Which region had the highest sales by year?
- Which are the total sales for each category by region and year?
- Who is your best performing sales person by year?

Normally, it would take you several iterations to come up with the calculations. However, with Pivot Tables, this is a breeze.

Let's address each question one by one:

Which region had the highest sales by year?

Step 1 - Click on **Insert**, **Pivot Table**

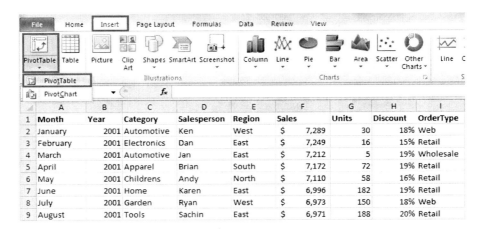

Figure 125

Step 2 - Make the data selection and **Click OK**

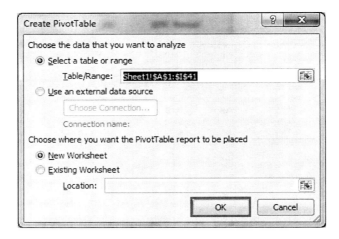

Figure 126

You will see something like this.

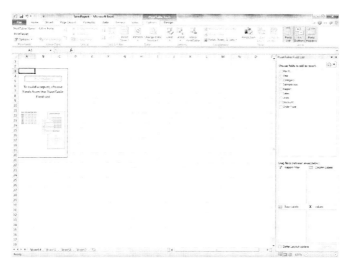

Figure 127

Step 3 - Make your selections by checking and un-checking the boxes and then dragging and dropping the fields in section Row Labels and Column Labels.

You may ask if we are going to drag and drop the field until we get the answers we are looking for. For the first question, which region had the highest sales by year?

Here is the output:

Figure 128

We can quickly see the answer for 2001 and it was the East Region which was the highest. And in 2002, it was the South Region.

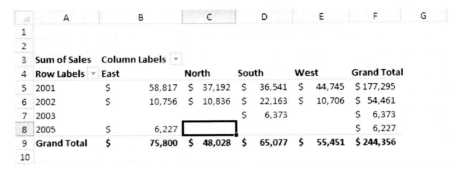

	A	B	C	D	E	F	G
1							
2							
3	Sum of Sales	Column Labels					
4	Row Labels	East	North	South	West	Grand Total	
5	2001	$ 58,817	$ 37,192	$ 36,541	$ 44,745	$ 177,295	
6	2002	$ 10,756	$ 10,836	$ 22,163	$ 10,706	$ 54,461	
7	2003			$ 6,373		$ 6,373	
8	2005	$ 6,227				$ 6,227	
9	Grand Total	$ 75,800	$ 48,028	$ 65,077	$ 55,451	$ 244,356	
10							

Figure 129

To answer our other questions, we check and uncheck the required fields and get the desired output. Here is a different view of the same data:

3	Sum of Sales	Column Labels					
4	Row Labels		2001	2002	2003	2005	Grand Total
5	East	$	58,817	$ 10,756		$6,227	$ 75,800
6	North	$	37,192	$ 10,836			$ 48,028
7	South	$	36,541	$ 22,163	$ 6,373		$ 65,077
8	West	$	44,745	$ 10,706			$ 55,451
9	Grand Total	$	177,295	$ 54,461	$ 6,373	$6,227	$ 244,356

Figure 130

Which are the total sales for each category by region and year?

Figure 131

78

Here is the output:

Sum of Sales	Column Labels				
Row Labels	2001	2002	2003	2005	Grand Total
East	$ 58,817	$10,756		$ 6,227	$ 75,800
Apparel				$ 6,227	$ 6,227
Automotive	$ 7,212	$ 5,444			$ 12,656
Electronics	$ 19,945	$ 5,312			$ 25,257
Garden	$ 5,762				$ 5,762
Home	$ 18,927				$ 18,927
Tools	$ 6,971				$ 6,971
North	$ 37,192	$10,836			$ 48,028
Automotive	$ 11,345				$ 11,345
Automtive	$ 6,361				$ 6,361
Childrens	$ 7,110				$ 7,110
Electronics		$ 5,502			$ 5,502
Garden		$ 5,334			$ 5,334
Toys	$ 12,376				$ 12,376
South	$ 36,541	$22,163	$ 6,373		$ 65,077
Apparel	$ 7,172				$ 7,172
Automotive	$ 5,842				$ 5,842
Childrens		$ 5,357			$ 5,357
Electronics	$ 11,697		$ 6,373		$ 18,070
Garden		$ 6,149			$ 6,149
Home		$ 5,345			$ 5,345
Tools	$ 11,830	$ 5,312			$ 17,142
West	$ 44,745	$10,706			$ 55,451
Apparel	$ 5,807	$ 5,410			$ 11,217
Automotive	$ 14,033				$ 14,033
Childrens	$ 11,983				$ 11,983
Garden	$ 6,973				$ 6,973
Toys	$ 5,949	$ 5,296			$ 11,245
Grand Total	$ 177,295	$54,461	$ 6,373	$ 6,227	$ 244,356

Figure 132

Who is your best performing sales person by year? Just move the Sales Person to the Row and Year in the Column and Sales in the Data area to get the answer.

Note I have included two table level drop-downs. So, if you wanted to see regional reports, you would just click on drop down arrows to see, for example, top sales person by year for 2001 and 2002 by region, or by region and category, etc.

I have just touched the proverbial tip of the iceberg on the power of Pivot Tables. There are numerous books on Pivot Tables alone and it is best left to the user to explore all the options. There are literally a hundred books by Microsoft MVPs and other Microsoft Excel experts on the topic if you wish to explore further. Just trust me, you will love pivot tables.

49. Sorting

Sorting is a basic command in Microsoft Excel and can be a powerful tool in helping you analyze your data by sorting alphabetically, or by high to low, or by a custom sort that you define. You can sort on any column. Here are the basics:

Step 1 - Click on **Data** and **Sort**

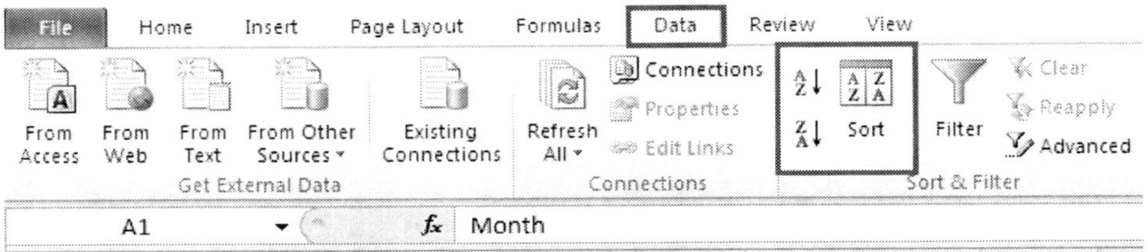

	A	B	C	D	E	F	G	H
1	Month	Year	Category	SalesPerson	Sales	Units	Region	
2	January	2008	Automotive	Jan	$3,090.97	73	East	
3	February	2008	Home	Wendy	$6,266.62	46	East	
4	March	2008	Electronics	Keith	$8,321.23	67	West	
5	April	2008	Automotive	Ryan	$1,073.49	2	Central	
6	May	2008	Home	Ryan	$6,828.44	7	Central	

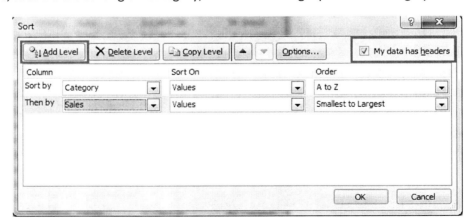

Figure 133

Step 2 - If your data has header rows, just check the box to let Microsoft Excel know to exclude that row from the sorting exercise. If you want multiple levels of sorting, click on **Add Level**. In this case, first we are sorting on Category, and within Category we are sorting by Sales.

Figure 134

You can experiment with the various options and set your own sorting criteria. Sort may be the best command to accomplish multi-level sorting of data.

50. Auto Fill

In Auto Fill, you drag the fill handle next to a number to easily create a number series.

By dragging the fill handle of a cell, you can copy the contents of that cell, including formulas, to other cells in the same row or column.

If the cell contains a number, date or time period that Microsoft Excel can project in a series, the values are incremented instead of copied. For example, if the cell contains "January," you can quickly fill in other cells in a row or column with "February," "March," and so on. You can also create a custom fill series for frequently used text entries, such as your company's sales regions.

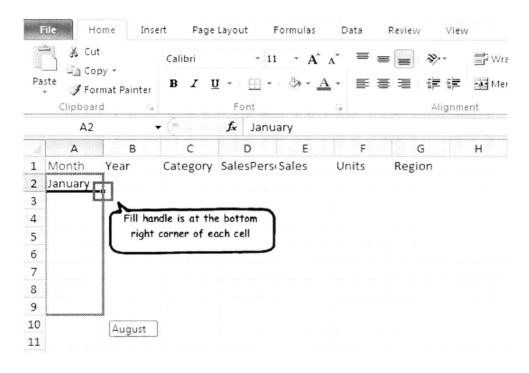

Figure 135

Automatically fill data

You can double-click the fill handle of a selected cell to fill the contents of the cell down a column for the same number of rows as the adjacent column. For example, if you type data in cells A1:A20, type a formula or text in cell B1, press **ENTER**, and then double-click the fill handle. Microsoft Excel fills the data down the column from cell B1 to cell B20.

51. Create a new worksheet / copy a worksheet

Since the goal of this book is to add productivity to your day-to-day tasks you can insert a new Microsoft Excel worksheet by pressing **SHIFT+F11**.

To select an entire sheet click on the corner between Column A and Row 1 as shown below

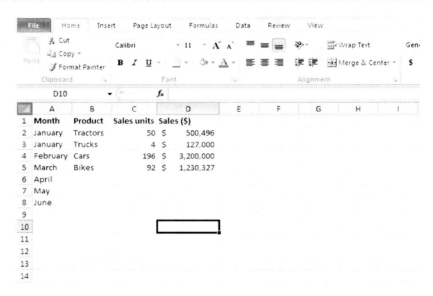

Figure 136

To copy the entire sheet selection and paste it onto a new tab or new workbook, you can use **CTRL+ C** to copy and **CTRL+ V** in the new sheet.

52. Quick Chart

With one keystroke, you can create a new chart or worksheet. To quickly create a chart, select the chart data, and then press **F11**. Let's say you have this data:

	A	B
1	**Month**	**Unit Sales**
2	January	200
3	February	300
4	March	400
5	April	500
6	May	350
7	June	375

Figure 137

To quickly chart it, select the data and just hit **F11**. Here is the default chart that is produced:

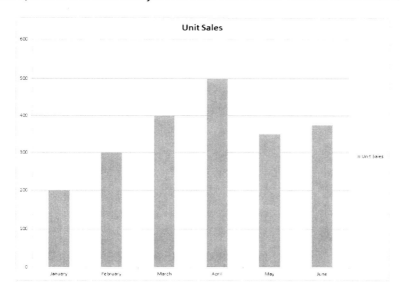

Figure 138

It is produced as its own new work sheet, as "Chart1" in this case.

You can move the chart to either your worksheet or another sheet by selecting the **Move Chart** button in the Excel ribbon:

Figure 139

The Move Chart button gives you the option to either place in as a new sheet or as an object in an existing sheet:

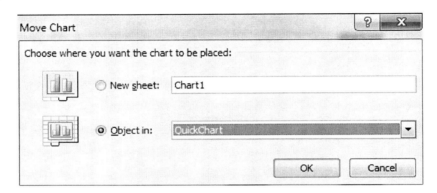

Figure 140

53. Insert Current Time/ Date Quickly

To quickly insert the Date or Time in an Excel spreadsheet:

Current date: Press **CTRL+SEMICOLON**

Current time: Press **CTRL+SHIFT+ SEMICOLON**

Current date and time: Press **CTRL+ SEMICOLON** then **SPACE + CTRL+SHIFT+ SEMICOLON**

54. Jump to Last Row/ Column in Table with Double-Click

Select any cell in the table and double-click on the cell-border in the direction you want to go:

	A	B	C
1	Item	Price	Quanity
2	Paint	$ 22.95	2
3	Paint Rollers	$ 6.95	4
4	Masking tape	$ 4.95	5
5	Sandpaper	$ 0.95	10
6	Caulking	$ 3.95	2
7	Mixing Brush	$ 5.95	1
8	Wire Brushes	$ 1.95	2

Figure 141

Double-click on A2 border if you want to go to last cell in the column:

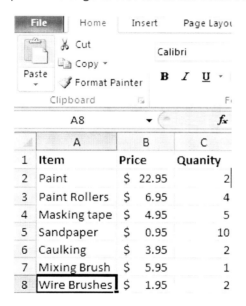

Figure 142

Fast Scroll

To quickly go to the last occupied cell of a row or column, select a cell and hit **CTRL and Down Arrow** to go the last row of the column. **CTRL+ →** for the last column in a row and so on.

55.Excel Sparklines

Excel Sparklines are a way to visualize data within a cell, versus using a separate chart. It is very useful when your job involves a lot of data analysis and sharing vast datasets, and is a quick way to summarize data trends by column or by row. Here are the steps to create Sparklines for columns of data:

Step 1 – Enter the data in a row or column. In this case, sales of a book by week.

	A	B	C
1	Book Sales by Week		
2	Week	Sales (Units)	
3	Week 1	5	
4	Week 2	12	
5	Week 3	40	
6	Week 4	75	
7	Week 5	65	
8	Week 6	24	
9	Week 7	82	
10	Week 8	36	
11	Week 9	44	
12	Week 10	28	
13			

Figure 143

Step 2 – Click on Insert and select Column Chart under Sparklines:

Figure 144

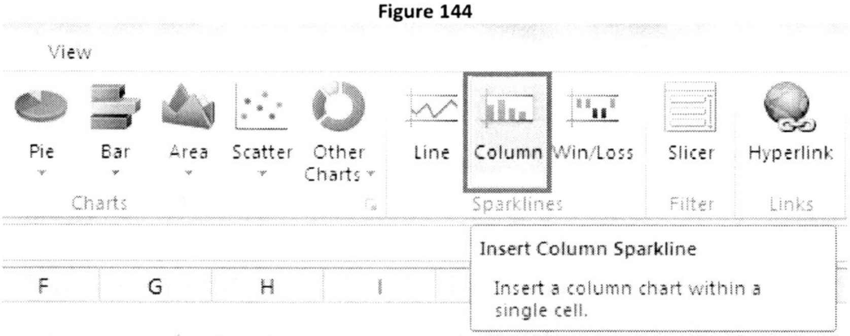

View

Pie Bar Area Scatter Other Charts ▾ | Line Column Win/Loss | Slicer Hyperlink

Charts | Sparklines | Filter Links

Insert Column Sparkline

Insert a column chart within a single cell.

Figure 145

Step 3 – Click on the Column chart and make the data selection. Also select the destination cell for the chart, which is usually going to be the cell at the end of your data, and click OK.

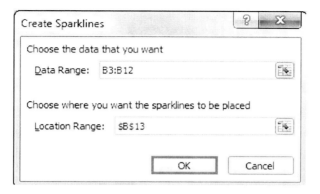

Figure 146

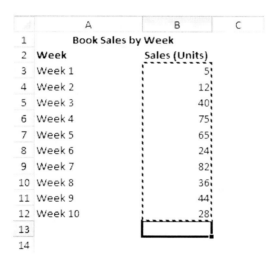

Figure 147

Step 4 – You will see the column chart in the destination cell B13, as shown below. Imagine how easy it will be to now visually analyze the data for each of several columns.

	A	B	C
1	Book Sales by Week		
2	Week	Sales (Units)	
3	Week 1	5	
4	Week 2	12	
5	Week 3	40	
6	Week 4	75	
7	Week 5	65	
8	Week 6	24	
9	Week 7	82	
10	Week 8	36	
11	Week 9	44	
12	Week 10	28	
13		▁▁▁▁▁	
14			

Figure 148

If you want to change the color of the chart, select the cell with the chart, go to the Design tab, and select Sparkline Color to change the color of the chart.

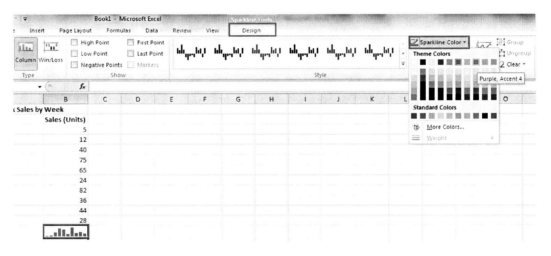

Figure 149

A column chart is good for representing data in a column, such as the above. For data in a row, it may be more useful to use a line chart. Use the steps above, and under Sparklines, choose Line Chart instead of Column Chart. This will give you a trend line representing the data in that row.

56. Jump to Any Spreadsheet

Right-click on the worksheet navigation arrows (bottom left) and you can go straight to any worksheet. This is very handy for workbooks with a lot of worksheets and is much faster than scrolling.

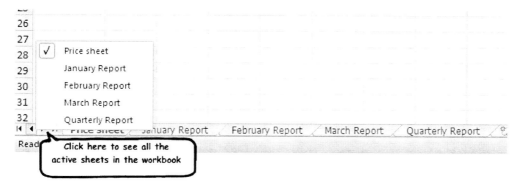

Figure 150

Right-clicking on the status bar about 1/4 away from the right–hand edge gives you the count, sum and average of your selection. The currently highlighted range is illustrated below:

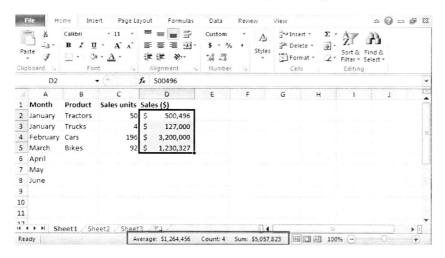

Figure 151

57. Freeze Panes

This command can save time in your day-to-day work and improve productivity, especially with large spreadsheets. Let's say you have a spreadsheet with 60 rows and 10 columns. The moment you start scrolling across, you may forget the column or row name and have to scroll back and forth to make sure you are editing the right cell. The solution is **Freeze Panes**. Here is how it works.

Let's say you have this spreadsheet:

	Month	Year	Category	Salesperson	Region	Sales		Units	Discount	OrderType
1	Month	Year	Category	Salesperson	Region	Sales		Units	Discount	OrderType
2	January	2001	Automotive	Ken	West	$	7,289	30	18%	Web
3	February	2001	Electronics	Dan	East	$	7,249	16	15%	Retail
4	March	2001	Automotive	Jan	East	$	7,212	5	19%	Wholesale
5	April	2001	Apparel	Brian	South	$	7,172	72	19%	Retail
6	May	2001	Childrens	Andy	North	$	7,110	58	16%	Retail
7	June	2001	Home	Karen	East	$	6,996	182	19%	Retail
8	July	2001	Garden	Ryan	West	$	6,973	150	18%	Web
9	August	2001	Tools	Sachin	East	$	6,971	188	20%	Retail
10	September	2001	Electronics	Amitabh	East	$	6,868	185	16%	Retail
11	October	2001	Toys	Kris	North	$	6,806	156	19%	Web
12	November	2001	Automotive	Dey	West	$	6,744	186	18%	Wholesale
13	December	2003	Electronics	Taylor	South	$	6,373	175	14%	Wholesale
14	January	2001	Automtive	Tom	North	$	6,361	202	19%	Phone
15	February	2005	Apparel	Karen	East	$	6,227	159	19%	Phone
16	March	2001	Childrens	Ken	West	$	6,215	190	15%	Phone
17	April	2001	Home	Karen	East	$	6,167	176	8%	Web
18	May	2002	Garden	Taylor	South	$	6,149	140	19%	Retail
19	June	2001	Tools	Brian	South	$	6,111	188	14%	Retail
20	July	2001	Electronics	Kory	South	$	6,080	189	19%	Web
21	August	2001	Toys	Ken	West	$	5,949	151	13%	Phone
22	September	2001	Automotive	Brian	South	$	5,842	80	18%	Phone
23	October	2001	Electronics	Dan	East	$	5,823	188	16%	Wholesale
24	November	2001	Automotive	George	North	$	5,825	138	16%	Phone
25	December	2001	Apparel	Patricia	West	$	5,807	185	14%	Phone
26	January	2001	Childrens	Ken	West	$	5,768	131	15%	Phone
27	February	2001	Home	Amitabh	East	$	5,764	179	15%	Retail

Figure 152

The window can only accommodate say 30 rows in this case:

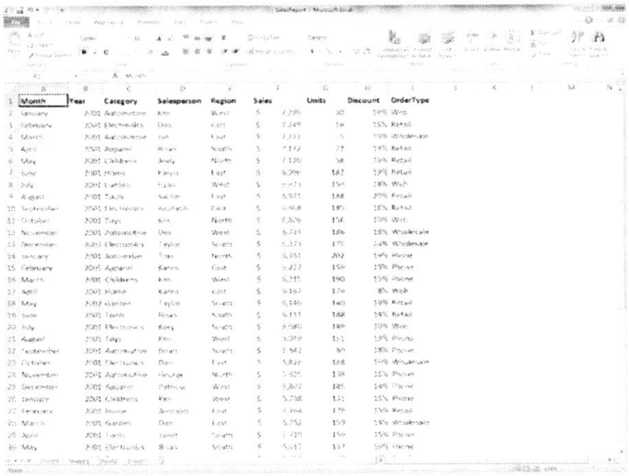

Figure 153

The moment you scroll down to row 33 or higher, you lose the column Titles. To avoid that from happening, freeze the top row:

Step 1 – Put your cursor where you want it, usually cell B2 to freeze both the columns and rows
Step 2 - Click on **View Tab**
Step 3 - **Freeze Panes** and select an option. You can freeze both rows and columns or just top rows or just the first column, depending on where the cursor is

Figure 154

58.Quick Close

Double-click on the Microsoft Excel Icon in 2010 to Close Microsoft Excel.

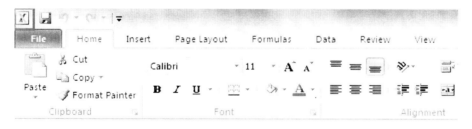

Figure 155

It's that simple. The dialog displays "Do you want to save the changes you made to "YourFileName.xlsx?"

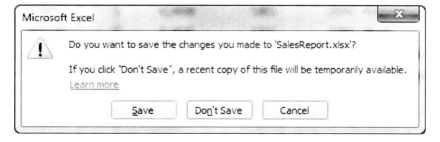

Figure 156

59. Automatically Adjust Column Width

Adjust column widths by selecting multiple columns and double clicking on the separators. This trick also works if you want to adjust row heights as well. You can select multiple columns (or rows) to adjust them at the same time.

	A	B	C	D	E
1	Item	Price	Quanity	Total	
2	Paint	$ 22.95	2	$ 45.90	
3	Paint Rolle	$ 6.95	4	$ 27.80	
4	Masking ta	$ 4.95	5	$ 24.75	
5	Sandpaper	$ 0.95	10	$ 9.50	
6	Caulking	$ 3.95	2	$ 7.90	
7	Mixing Bru	$ 5.95	1	$ 5.95	
8	Wire Brush	$ 1.95	2	$ 3.90	

Figure 157

60. Format Numbers in a Cell

To quickly format the numbers in a cell, select the cell and hit **CTRL+1**:

	A	B	C	D	E
1	Item	Price	Quanity	Total	
2	Paint	$ 22.95	2	$ 45.90	
3	Paint Rolle	$ 6.95	4	$ 27.80	
4	Masking ta	$ 4.95	5	$ 24.75	
5	Sandpaper	$ 0.95	10	$ 9.50	
6	Caulking	$ 3.95	2	$ 7.90	
7	Mixing Bru	$ 5.95	1	$ 5.95	
8	Wire Brush	$ 1.95	2	$ 3.90	
9					

Figure 158

You will see the formatting window where you can select the option that apply to the cell.

Figure 159

Here are some useful tips to format a cell quickly:

- CTRL+SHIFT+~ - Applies the General number format.
- CTRL+SHIFT+$ - Applies the Currency format with two decimal places.
- CTRL+SHIFT+% - Applies the Percentage format with no decimal places.

61. Hide and Unhide Sheet

Often when working on group projects or monthly or yearly planning reports, you end up with various versions of work tabs for different scenarios. When you are sharing the spreadsheet with your team member you may want to keep all tabs in the same spreadsheet (so that you are not maintaining versions of your work in different places), yet show only the active tabs to your team members.

Fortunately, Excel provides a cool feature called **Hide Worksheet**. Only you know that your original versions are "hidden" and you can refer to them anytime. It is better than password-protected sheets since most often everyone should have access to the raw data if they need to.

Hiding a particular tab or spreadsheet is pretty simple:

Step 1 - Click on **Format** in the **Home** Tab

Figure 160

Step 2 - Click on **Hide and Unhide** under Visibility

Step 3 - Select **Hide Sheet**

Figure 161

94

Step 4 - The active sheet will be hidden

You can hide multiple sheets by holding down the **Ctrl key** selecting multiple tabs at one time.

Figure 162

If you want to unhide:

Step 1 - Go to any sheet

Step 2 - Click on **Format** in the **Home** tab

Figure 163

Step 3- Under **Visibility** select **Hide & Unhide**

Step 4 - Click on **Unhide Sheet**

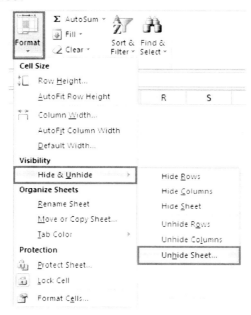

Figure 164

On clicking it will launch a window of all hidden sheets in this case, for example, sales data

Unhide
Unhide sheet:
SalesData
OK
Cancel

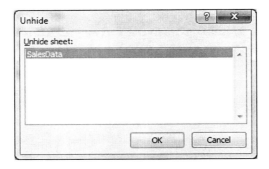

Figure 165

Step 5 - Click **OK** and the sheet will appear

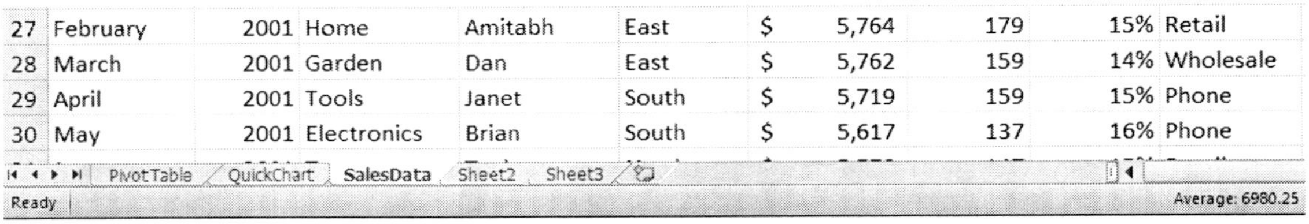

27 February 2001 Home Amitabh East $ 5,764 179 15% Retail
28 March 2001 Garden Dan East $ 5,762 159 14% Wholesale
29 April 2001 Tools Janet South $ 5,719 159 15% Phone
30 May 2001 Electronics Brian South $ 5,617 137 16% Phone
PivotTable
QuickChart
SalesData
Sheet2
Sheet3
Ready
Average: 6980.25

Figure 166

The other way to hide and unhide a spreadsheet is to right-click on the tab of an active sheet and click on **Hide**.

Insert...
Delete
Rename
Move or Copy...
View Code
Protect Sheet...
Tab Color
Hide
Unhide...
Select All Sheets

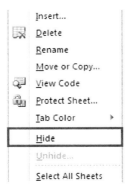

Figure 167

To unhide, right-click on any other active sheet and click **Unhide**

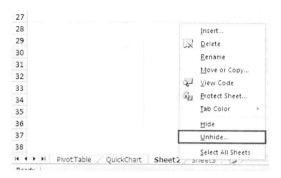

Figure 168

62. Transpose - Convert Rows to Columns or Vice Versa

Let's say someone sent you a spreadsheet with the data laid out as follows, with months going across and all subsequent information like "SalesPerson" and "Sales" also going across.

	A	B	C	D	E	F	G	H	I	J	K	L	M	N
1	**Month**	January	February	March	April	May	June	July	August	September	October	November	December	January
2	**Year**	2001	2001	2001	2001	2001	2001	2001	2001	2001	2001	2001	2003	2001
3	**Category**	Automotive	Electronics	Automotive	Apparel	Childrens	Home	Garden	Tools	Electronics	Toys	Automotive	Electronics	Automtive
4	**Salesperson**	Ken	Dan	Jan	Brian	Andy	Karen	Ryan	Sachin	Amitabh	Kris	Dey	Taylor	Tom
5	**Sales**	$ 7,289	$ 7,249	$ 7,212	$7,172	$ 7,110	$6,996	$6,973	$6,971	$ 6,868	$6,806	$ 6,744	$ 6,373	$ 6,361

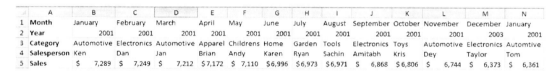

Figure 169

If you instead prefer to consume the information with months going down the rows, you could use **Transpose**. It is a very handy feature. Here is how it works:

Step 1 - Select all the cells you want to transpose

	A	B	C	D	E	F	G	H	I	J	K	L	M	N	O	P	Q	R
1	Month	January	February	March	April	May	June	July	August	September	October	November	December	January	February	March	April	May
2	Year	2001	2001	2001	2001	2001	2001	2001	2001	2001	2001	2001	2003	2001	2005	2001	2001	2002
3	Category	Automotive	Electronics	Automotive	Apparel	Childrens	Home	Garden	Tools	Electronics	Toys	Automotive	Electronics	Automtive	Apparel	Childrens	Home	Garden
4	Salesperson	Ken	Dan	Jan	Brian	Andy	Karen	Ryan	Sachin	Amitabh	Kris	Dey	Taylor	Tom	Karen	Ken	Karen	Taylor
5	Sales	$ 7,289	$ 7,249	$ 7,212	$7,172	$ 7,110	$6,996	$6,973	$6,971	$ 6,868	$6,806	$ 6,744	$ 6,373	$ 6,361	$ 6,227	$ 6,215	$6,167	$6,149

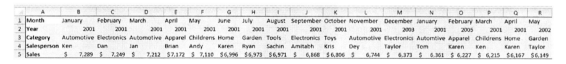

Figure 170

Step 2 - Go to the first empty cell

Step 3 - Right-click and Select Paste Special

Step 4 - Select **Transpose**

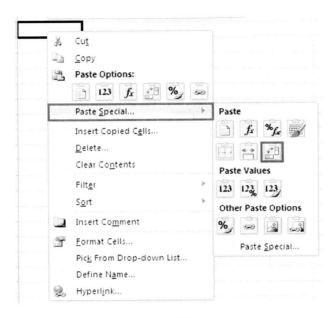

Figure 171

You can select from either the 4th option under **Paste Options** or the **Transpose** from the pop-out menu under **Paste.**

Step 5 - Your data is now converted into your desired format

	A	B	C	D	E	F	G	H	I
1	**Month**	January	February	March	April	May	June	July	August
2	**Year**	2001	2001	2001	2001	2001	2001	2001	2001
3	**Category**	Automotive	Electronics	Automotive	Apparel	Childrens	Home	Garden	Tools
4	**Salesperson**	Ken	Dan	Jan	Brian	Andy	Karen	Ryan	Sachin
5	**Sales**	$ 7,289	$ 7,249	$ 7,212	$7,172	$ 7,110	$6,996	$6,973	$6,971
6									
7	**Month**	**Year**		**Category**	**Salesperson**	**Sales**			
8	January	2001	Automotive	Ken	$7,289				
9	February	2001	Electronics	Dan	$7,249				
10	March	2001	Automotive	Jan	$7,212				
11	April	2001	Apparel	Brian	$7,172				
12	May	2001	Childrens	Andy	$7,110				
13	June	2001	Home	Karen	$6,996				
14	July	2001	Garden	Ryan	$6,973				
15	August	2001	Tools	Sachin	$6,971				
16	September	2001	Electronics	Amitabh	$6,868				
17	October	2001	Toys	Kris	$6,806				
18	November	2001	Automotive	Dey	$6,744				
19	December	2003	Electronics	Taylor	$6,373				
20	January	2001	Automtive	Tom	$6,361				
21	February	2005	Apparel	Karen	$6,227				
22	March	2001	Childrens	Ken	$6,215				
23	April	2001	Home	Karen	$6,167				
24	May	2002	Garden	Taylor	$6,149				
25	June	2001	Tools	Brian	$6,111				
26	July	2001	Electronics	Kory	$6,080				
27	August	2001	Toys	Ken	$5,949				
28	September	2001	Automotive	Brian	$5,842				
29	October	2001	Electronics	Dan	$5,828				
30	November	2001	Automotive	George	$5,825				
31	December	2001	Apparel	Patricia	$5,807				
32	January	2001	Childrens	Ken	$5,768				
33	February	2001	Home	Amitabh	$5,764				
34	March	2001	Garden	Dan	$5,762				
35									
36									

Figure 172

Microsoft Word® 2010

Microsoft Word 2010 is a word processing program, designed to help you create professional-quality documents. With Microsoft Word, you can not only edit, revise, and format your documents, but also easily collaborate with others. No single book can cover the breadth of the feature set for Microsoft Word; I am just including a small set that might enhance your productivity.

63. Blogging from Microsoft Word

One of the nice features in Microsoft Word 2010 is the ability to publish your blog directly from the application. Here are the steps required:

Step 1 - Create your blog posting in Microsoft Word:

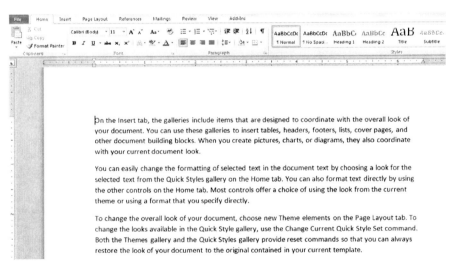

Figure 173

Step 2 - Click on **File, Save & Send** then the **Publish as Blog Post**, Publish as a Blog post **button**

Document1 - Microsoft Word
File
Home
Insert
Page Layout
References
Mailings
Review
View
Add-Ins
Save
Save As
Open
Close
Info
Recent
New
Print
Save & Send
Help
Options
Exit
Save & Send
Send Using E-mail
Save to Web
Save to SharePoint
Publish as Blog Post
File Types
Change File Type
Create PDF/XPS Document
Publish as Blog Post
Create a new blog post using the current document. Blogging is a way to publish content to the Web or within an organization.
Some supported blogging sites include:
SharePoint Blog
WordPress
Blogger
Windows Live Spaces
Community Server
TypePad
You will be prompted to register your blog account if this is the first time you have a published a blog post from Word. You may add additional blog accounts or change existing blog accounts at any time.
Publish as Blog Post

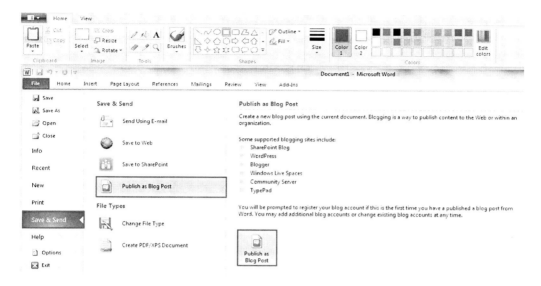

Figure 174

Enter Blog Post Title in the Grey section:

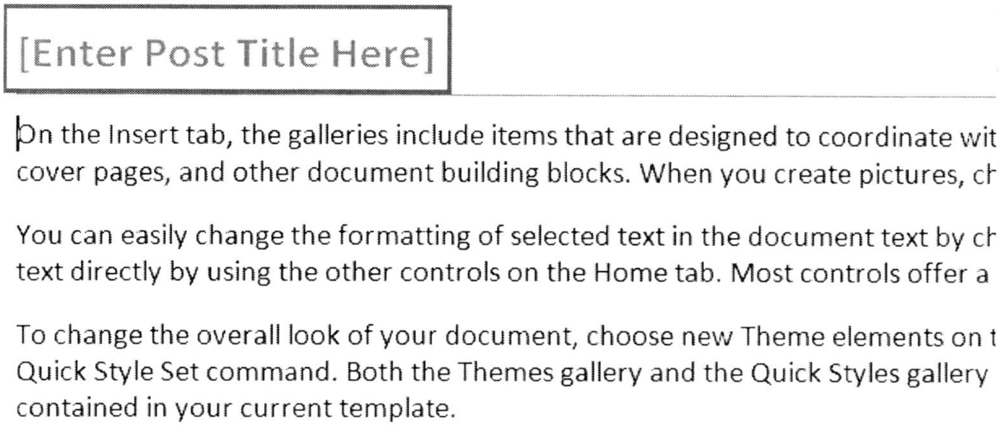

[Enter Post Title Here]
On the Insert tab, the galleries include items that are designed to coordinate wit
cover pages, and other document building blocks. When you create pictures, ch
You can easily change the formatting of selected text in the document text by ch
text directly by using the other controls on the Home tab. Most controls offer a
To change the overall look of your document, choose new Theme elements on t
Quick Style Set command. Both the Themes gallery and the Quick Styles gallery
contained in your current template.

Figure 175

Step 3 - Click on **Publish** button

Figure 176

Step 4 - Enter your blog user name and password, and you're done!

Figure 177

There is a prerequisite to this step, which is associating your blog account with Word:

Step 5 - Click on **Manage Accounts**

Figure 178

You will be prompted for Blog Accounts – click **New**

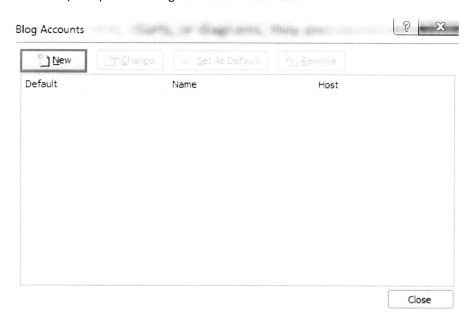

Figure 179

Step 6 - Select your blog provider

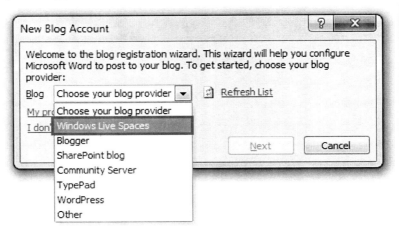

Figure 180

Step 7 - Click on **Next**

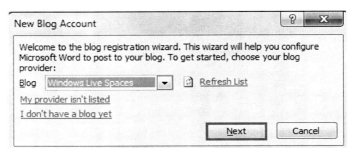

Figure 181

Step 8 - Enter your blog account credentials and you're all set

Figure 182

64. Look up a Word in the Thesaurus

When you press **Shift + F7**, if the cursor is on a word, it will highlight that word and automatically look it up in the thesaurus.

A related but useful command is **Alt+7** which takes you to **Next Misspelling** while running a spell check in a document.

65.Save As and Auto recover

This might sound silly, but sometimes this simple command can be a real lifesaver.

Ctrl + SHIFT + S will save your file, and is very helpful if you want to quickly save a version of your current document, or save it to your flash drive.

I recommend setting your AutoRecover option to save your document every 2 minutes. To set this:

Step 1 - Click on **File, Options**

Figure 183

Step 2 - Click on **Save,** Save **AutoRecover** information every 2 minutes or any other interval you prefer.

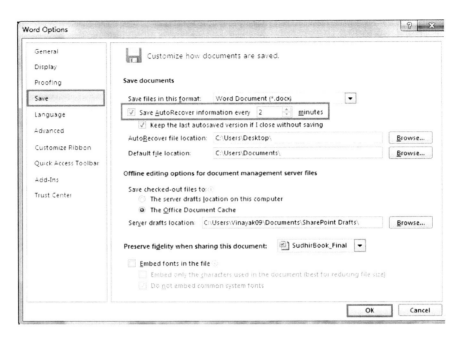

Figure 184

66. Pick Up Where You Left Off

You don't have to leave a document open; type in **Shift+F5**, and the cursor will be back exactly where you left it. I can't tell you the value of this command to quickly recover the thought process in the event you were interrupted while working on a Word document. I recommend trying it right away.

Step 1 - Open an existing Microsoft Word document and scroll down midway.
Step 2 - Close it.
Step 3 – Open it again and press **Shift+F5**. The cursor will be where you left it when you closed the document.

67. Auto Correct

Though the spell checker in Word helps catch most typos, it cannot catch all of the technical terms unique to your field, or difficult names. So, the solution to that is AutoCorrect.

Let's assume we have a word, "technet," and the correct way to refer to it is TechNet. This is a minor but important difference from a brand and usage point of view. Here are the steps to use auto correct:

Step 1 - Type the word, into your document in this case "technet"
Step 2 - Right-click on the word

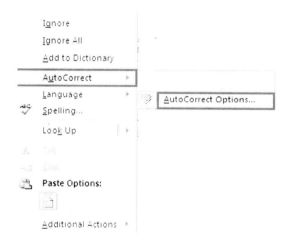

Figure 185

Step 3 - Type in **Replace**: technet with TechNet

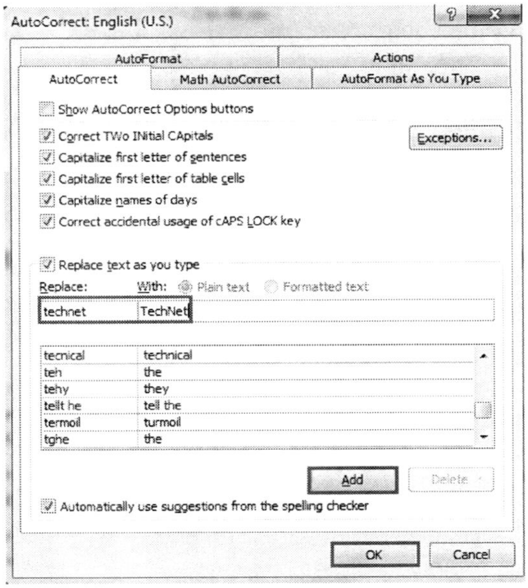

Figure 186

Step 4 - Click **Add**
Step 5 - Click **OK**

68. Change case

Sometimes you have to change the case of a text. For example, you may have to change the text of an entire sentence to upper case, or vice versa when you have accidentally hit the caps lock and have been typing without looking up.

Here are the steps:

Step 1 - TYPE A SENTENCE IN UPPER CASE
Step 2 - Select **All**
Step 3 - Hit **SHIFT+F3** and toggle through the options

69. Taking Screenshots within Microsoft Word

Microsoft Word 2010 has a feature that allows you to take screenshots of an existing window and insert it in the document. Here are the steps:

Step 1 - Click on **Screenshot** under the **Insert** tab

Figure 187

Step 2 - Select one of the **Active Windows** that you want a screenshot of

Figure 188

Step 3 - The image is embedded in your word document

Figure 189

70. Switching Between Document Pages

Here are the short cuts to switch between several pages in the same document:

- **Ctrl + Home**: Showing top of your document
- **Ctrl + Alt + End**: Showing end of your document
- **Shift + Page Up**: Page Up Extend
- **Shift + Page Down**: Page Down Extend

71. Page Breaks

You can insert page breaks quickly and easily by pressing the **Ctrl + ENTER** button. This is very useful if you have lots of pages to edit.

72. Send any document as a PDF

Sometimes when working with Microsoft Word documents, you want to share them in such a way that they cannot be edited or changed because of copyright issues or legal needs. So you may need to convert it to PDF. Now, the PDF version is built right into Word.

Here are the steps:

Step 1 - Click on **File, Save and Send**
Step 2 - Select **Create PDF/XPS Document**
Step 3 - Click on **Create PDF/XPS Button**

Figure 190

Step 4 - Save the file as a **PDF**

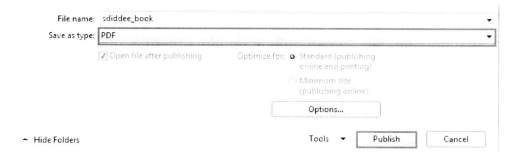

Figure 191

73. Captions in Microsoft Word

This is again one of those subtle enhancements which add to your productivity. Let's say you have an image that you want to provide a caption for. In this case, I have taken the home page of Bing and need to add a caption to it.

Figure 192

Here are the steps:

Step 1 - Select the image

Step 2 - Click on **References** Tab, **Insert Caption** Button

Figure 193

Step 3 - Add a Caption or use the default

Step 4 – Click **OK**

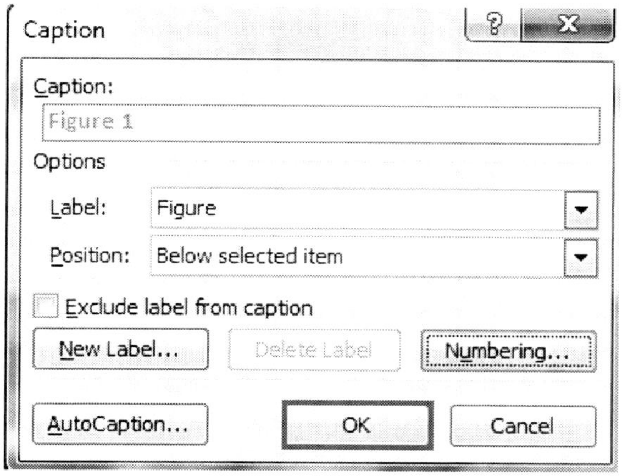

Figure 194

74. Artistic Effects

Sometimes you need to add a bit of pizzazz to your images. So let's say you have the Tip 73 caption dialog box

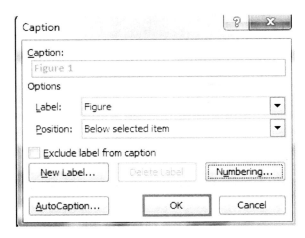

Figure 195

To add an Artistic Effect, follow these steps:

Step 1 - Click on an image

Step 2 - Click **Format**, **Artistic Effects**

Step 3 - Select the effect you want

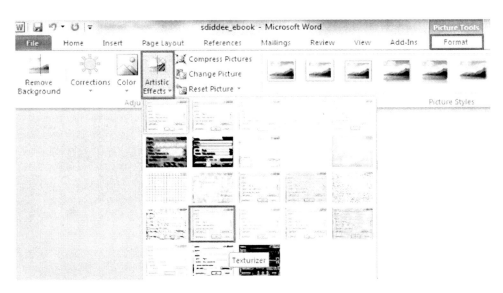

Figure 196

The output in this case looks like this:

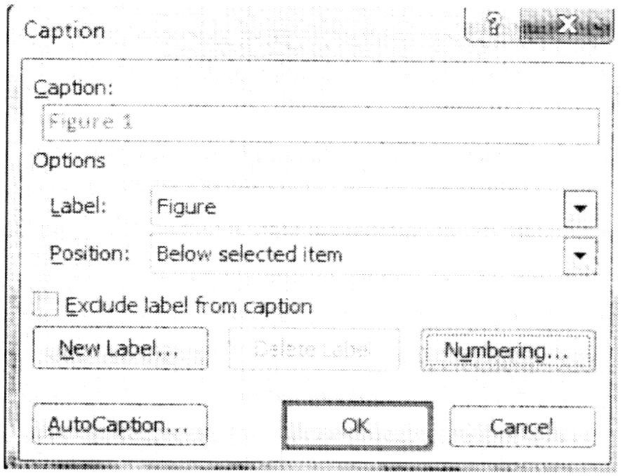

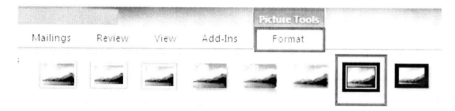

Figure 197

You can format it further by using various frame options by selecting the following:

Figure 198

Double Frame, Black, Soft Edge etc. I suggest you scroll through all the options to see which one appeals to you.

Figure 199

115

Figure 200

75. Subscript and Superscript

Select a word you want to convert to a subscript, and click **CTRL and "+="**

To convert a word to superscript click **CTRL+SHIFT and "+="**

Note: Use the key that has the + and = sign, next to backspace on most keyboards.

76. Create a Line Quickly

If you need to create a line in a document to separate sections, type the hyphen key three times and hit **ENTER.**

To create a double line type in "=" three time and hit **Enter.** To try other combinations follow the same steps and use * or tilde symbol for a designer line, "#" for a thick line with two thin lines etc.

77. Drag-and-drop Navigation Pane

This is one of the cooler features of Microsoft Word 2010. The Document Map gives you a view of headers and document sections, graphics, etc. In fact, this entire book relied on it as I worked through the formatting process. The navigation makes rearranging and organizing content really easy. Here are the steps to follow:

Click on the **View Tab** in the ribbon and Check the box labeled **Navigation Pane**.

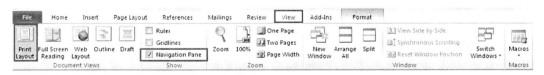

Figure 201

You can move whole sections of text by dragging and dropping the headings in the navigation pane. This works much better than the old "cut and paste" method.

Here is how the Navigation Pane of this book looks like.

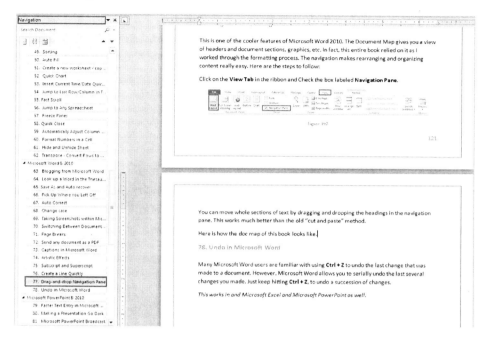

Figure 202

78. Undo in Microsoft Word

Many Microsoft Word users are familiar with using **Ctrl + Z** to undo the last change that was made to a document. However, Microsoft Word allows you to undo the last *several* changes you made. Just keep hitting **Ctrl + Z**, to undo a succession of changes.

This works in and Microsoft Excel and Microsoft PowerPoint as well.

Microsoft PowerPoint® 2010

Microsoft PowerPoint is used to create presentations to convey your ideas to small or large audiences. Many people in large companies often live in Microsoft PowerPoint because of the need to collaborate and work on complex ideas together. The next few tips are intended to save you time in Microsoft PowerPoint slides, or make you even more efficient at something in which you might already be very proficient.

79. Faster Text Entry in Microsoft PowerPoint

You can enter text into slides by hitting **CTRL+ENTER**. This is very useful when entering data in a slide deck. **CTRL +ENTER** moves to the first text box which is usually the TITLE slide. Entering **CTRL+ENTER** takes you to the next text box with bullets and more. At the end of last text box, **CTRL+ENTER** takes you to a new slide. This significantly cuts down time entering text.

80. Making a Presentation Go Dark

If you want an undivided attention of a room during a presentation, once in Slide Show mode, press **'B'**, which will make the screen go to black. To go back to the presentation, press **'B'** again.

If you want to turn the screen to white, simply press **'W'** while in Slide Show mode.

81. Microsoft PowerPoint Broadcast

Microsoft PowerPoint 2010 enables you to broadcast a presentation to others at remote locations whether or not they have PowerPoint installed on their computers. (The Broadcast Slide Show feature works with Microsoft SharePoint Server 2010 or Windows Live.)

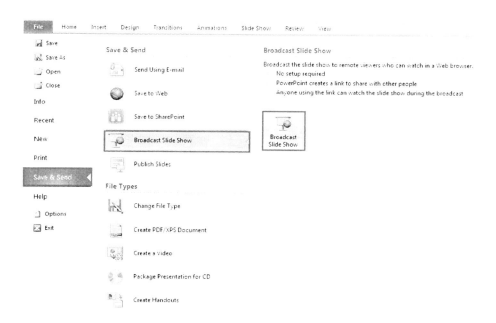

Figure 203

Or click on **Slide Show** and select **Broadcast Slide Show**

Figure 204

You can choose to start from any point in the presentation.

When prompted, select **"Start Broadcast"**:

Figure 205

The broadcast service sends your remote audience members the link to your presentation so they can log with their Windows Live account.

Please note that broadcasting your presentation in this way displays the visual portion of your presentation only; **no audio is transmitted**. If audio is necessary for your presentation, set up a conference call so that participants can hear your narration, ask questions, and participate in the presentation.

82. Show Grid Lines

Anyone who has had to make a complex slide has had to struggle with the complexity of fitting the text and images on the minimal space available and aligning with the other objects on the slide. One simple way to achieve this objective is to use **Grid Lines**.

120

On any slide, press **SHIFT+F9** to show the grid lines. Here is an example with the grid lines, making it easy to align the various objects on the slide.

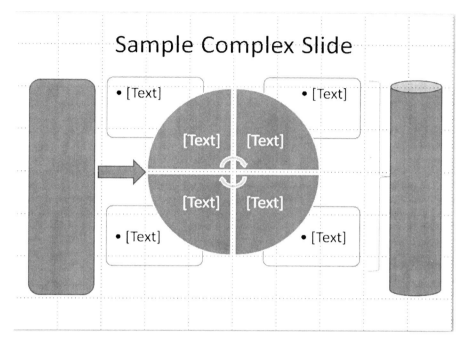

Figure 206

83. Pin Most-Used Presentations

If you are working on a presentation that you use very often, you can "pin" it so that you can access it quickly:

Step 1 - Go to **File**

Step 2 - Scroll down to **Recent**

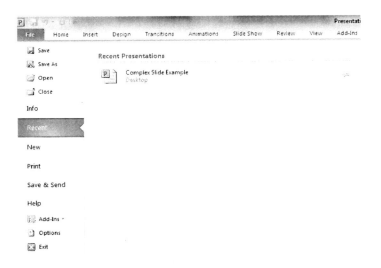

Figure 207

Step 3 - Click on the **Pin**

Figure 208

Your Presentation is now pinned for easy access next time you open Power Point, meaning it will not fall off your "Recent" list until you unpin it.

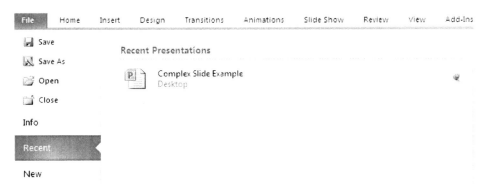

Figure 209

84. Create a presentation from an outline

It is rare that one presentation will contain the work of one person; most often people work in small groups to put together a slide deck. However, PowerPoint may not be the most efficient way to start a deck. The slide deck idea or outline of a presentation might have started as a brainstorming session, or meeting notes on what to present and why.

One of the cooler features of Microsoft PowerPoint 2010 is the ability to create a presentation from a Word document. Let's say you have an amazing idea to build a new application for smartphones. You quickly realize you will need to raise funding from venture capitalists. You brainstorm with your core group to come up with a Pitch Deck. Here is what the outline of your slide deck, will look like which is in a Microsoft Word document:

- Title
- Founders and Company background
- Customer Problem
- Proposed Solution
- Market Analysis and Market Opportunity
- Competitive Solutions
- Differentiators
- Business Model
- Project Milestones
- Current Partners and Pipeline
- Financial Model (Revenue, Expenses, Projections) & Funding Ask

To create a PowerPoint presentation from a Microsoft Word outline, here are the steps to follow:

Step 1 – Launch Microsoft PowerPoint 2010. Go to **File** and click on **New Slide** as shown

Figure 210

Step 2 – Click on Slides **from Outline** as shown below

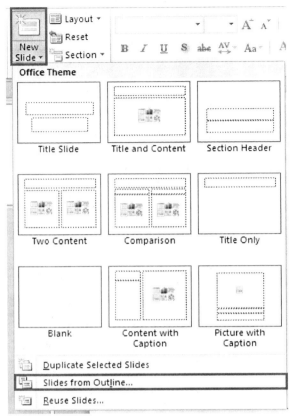

Figure 211

Step 3 – Browse to find the word document from which to create the slide deck. In this case, the document is called PitchDeck.docx and it is on the Desktop

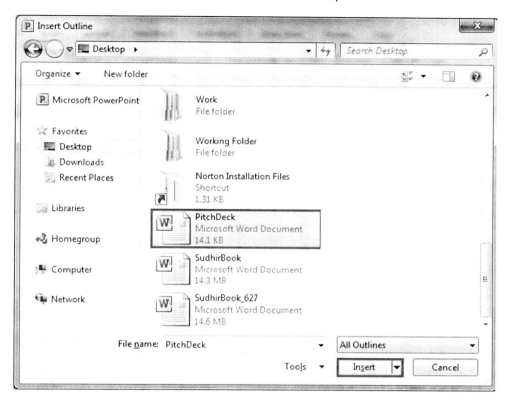

Figure 212

And your outline appears as a slide deck. Now you can work on your individual slides.

85. Using the Mouse as a Pointer

Since this book is all about productivity, this is one cool feature which can help anyone doing a presentation. Sometimes when you are presenting a slide with a lot of information to a group, it's difficult to guide your audience to a specific point in the slide. And to make matters worse, you don't have a laser pointer on you. Fortunately, there is a solution.

Step 1 – Launch the Microsoft PowerPoint Slideshow or **Reading View**
Step 2 – Click **CTRL+ Left click** on the mouse or touchpad

You should see a laser pointer on the screen!

Here is an example:

Highest Scorers in Indian Cricket

- Sachin Tendulkar
- Rahul Dravid ₀
- Sunil Gavaskar
- VVS Laxman
- V Sehwag

Figure 213

One less thing to worry about during presentations!

86. Draw a perfectly straight line in Microsoft PowerPoint

Many of us can identify with this pain point. You need to draw a straight or horizontal line in your slide.

Sounds simple, right? Unfortunately, it is not. When you try and select the line icon and draw a horizontal or vertical line, It is invariably skewed by the time you reach the desired dimension. Next you see yourself minutely moving the line till you feel it is as straight as it can be - until you project it on a big screen where the minutest error is magnified 10 fold!

There has to be an easy solution when you want a perfectly straight line. In fact, there is.

Step 1 -Select the Line Control on the Home Tab

Figure 214

Step 2 - Hold down the **Shift key** while you **left click** on the mouse and drag to draw the line using the line tool.

Step 3 - When you have the desired length of the line, release the mouse

Step 4 - Release the **Shift key**. Your line is ready.

Figure 215

87. Perfect shapes in Microsoft PowerPoint

If you spend a lot of times using shapes in Microsoft PowerPoint, you may notice that shapes will offer you an oval but not a circle or a rectangle but not a square. Just select **CTRL key** on your keyboard when selecting a shape and clicking. You will always start with the perfect circle, square, cylinder, triangle, star etc. that you can resize to meet your needs. This saves endless hours of making a shape presentation ready.

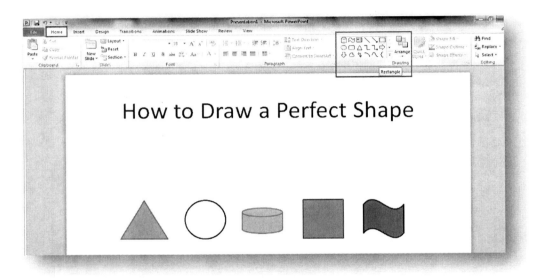

Figure 216

Microsoft OneNote® 2010

Microsoft OneNote (formerly called Microsoft Office OneNote) is a digital notebook on your computer. It is a single place where you can gather all of your notes and information, with the ability to search your notes, images etc. With these notebooks you can manage information overload and work together with others more effectively. Once you start using Microsoft OneNote and get comfortable with the features, it is unlikely you will go back to using a regular notebook for note taking or information gathering.

If you don't have Microsoft OneNote, go online and check out the features, to see if Microsoft OneNote is for you.

88. OneNote Tasks in Outlook

You can flag Microsoft OneNote items as Tasks to track in Microsoft Outlook (see Tip 39) with **Ctrl + Shift +1**. The task is created in Microsoft Outlook, and the done/not done status is kept in sync with Microsoft OneNote.

You create a task by Clicking **CTRL+SHIFT+1.**

Figure 217

It shows up in your task list in Microsoft Outlook automatically. Cool, huh?

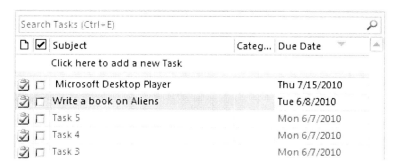

Figure 218

89. Microsoft OneNote in Full-Screen mode

If you are working on a notebook page and need more screen area, hit the **F11** key. See the difference in the two notes here? It always helps to de-clutter the screen and focus on the meeting or task at hand.

Normal Screen mode

Figure 219

Full screen mode

Figure 220

90. E-mail Notes

If you become addicted to Microsoft OneNote as I have, you will find yourself taking all your meeting notes in Microsoft OneNote, creating tasks and more. If you need to share the meeting notes by sending an e-mail consisting of the Microsoft OneNote page, hit **Ctrl + Shift + E**. Click the button in the toolbar, choose your recipients, and your notes are distributed without any retyping.

91. Screen Clipping

This is one of the cool features which makes Microsoft OneNote one of my favorite products. When you are on a website or a program and you want to capture a snippet of the site and file it for reference, you can capture screenshots of what you see. This is especially useful for Web research, trip planning, online shopping, and product comparisons.

Here are the steps:

Step 1 - Insert a screen clipping from the Web: Press **Windows Logo key + S while** in any program or browser.

Step 2 - Select an area of your screen. A separate Microsoft OneNote window will open to display the Unfiled Notes section where the screen clipping is inserted

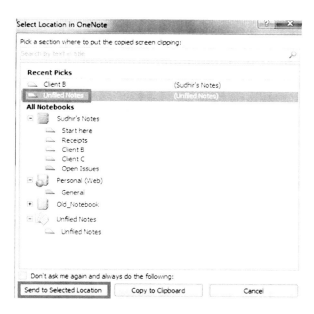

Figure 221

Here is how it is embedded:

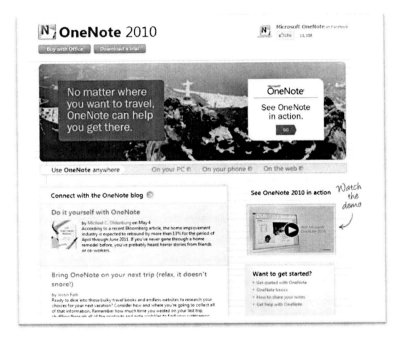

Figure 222

Microsoft OneNote 2010 - Planner and note taking software - Office.com
http://office.microsoft.com/en-us/onenote/
Screen clipping taken: 7/10/2011 10:08 AM

Hint: If you want to insert a screen clipping into the current page instead of the Unfiled Notes section, switch to the Microsoft OneNote window, put the cursor where you want the clipping, and click Insert > Screen Clipping or the Clip button on the toolbar:

Figure 223

92. Search within an Image

Microsoft OneNote can search within a screen image. How cool is that? Just click **CTRL + F**

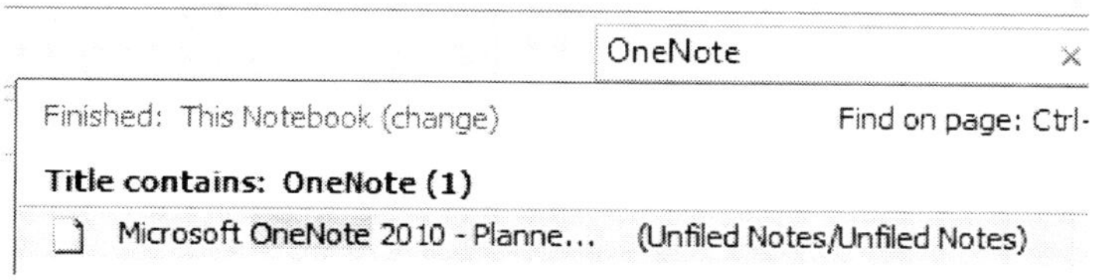

Figure 224

Here is how the results will appear:

Figure 225

93. Copy Text from a Picture

You can copy text from an image in Microsoft OneNote by right-clicking and selecting **Copy Text from Picture**

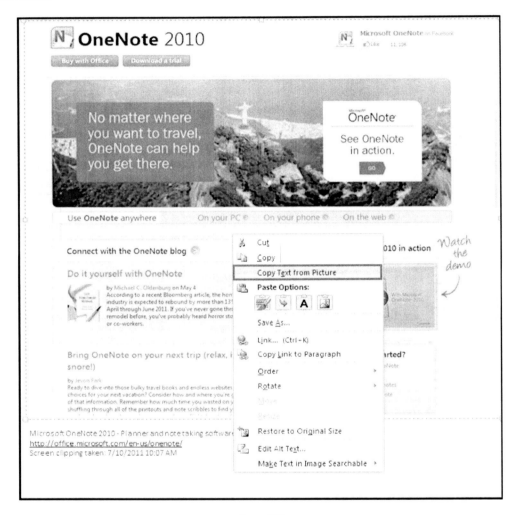

Figure 226

94. New Notes

You can use Microsoft OneNote alongside another program simultaneously. While in any other program or website, press:

Windows Logo key +N

Figure 227

to start a new Microsoft OneNote note, which can co-exist on the page. It you click on the One Note window and hit **CTRL+ALT+D** keys it automatically docks it to the right edge of the screen.

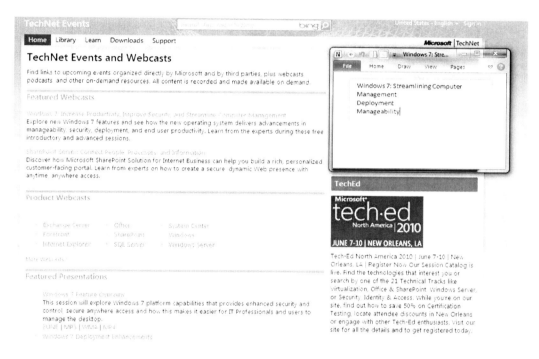

Figure 228

95. Linked Microsoft Outlook Meeting Notes

In any meeting, you can click on the Microsoft OneNote icon to create linked meeting notes

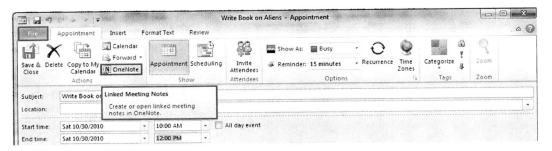

Figure 229

Clicking on the icon gives you an option to insert the notes into the right category

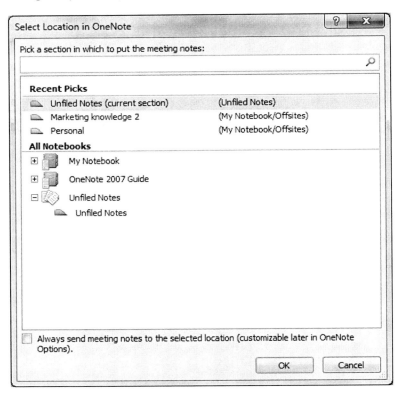

Figure 230

It automatically creates a note with the meeting title and all the attendees in the meeting.

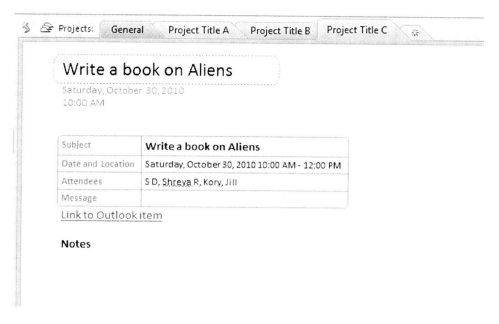

Figure 231

96. Perform Basic Calculations in Microsoft OneNote

Microsoft OneNote allows basic mathematical calculations, using the same symbols as Excel. Place the cursor after the = (equal) sign in each example below and press the spacebar:

3*9=

54/6=

For those who have not used formulas much * is for multiplication and / is for division etc.

97. Insert Microsoft OneNote Tables "on the fly"

Sometimes when you are taking notes, you need to insert a table to capture information in a grid. Type in your text and hit the **Tab key**. A table will magically appear—and if you hit tab, you can add additional columns.

When you want to create a row, just hit enter:

Write a book on Aliens
Saturday, October 30, 2010
10:00 AM

Subject	Write a book on Aliens
Date and Location	Saturday, October 30, 2010 10:00 AM - 12:00 PM
Attendees	Sudhir Diddee, Shreya R, Kory, Jill M., S Mehrotra, R.Shankar
Message	

Link to Outlook item

Notes

Action Item	Due Date	Owner	Notes

Figure 232

98. Quick Bullets in Microsoft OneNote

If you want to have bullet points in your notes, you can just type **CTRL + the period key "."** The text appears as a bulleted list. If you want the list to appear as numbers instead of bullets, type **CTRL + the slash key "/"**.If you want to indent, hit the **Tab** key.

99. Attach Files to Microsoft OneNote

You can store documents and other files directly on a Microsoft OneNote page, which comes in very handy if you are trying to keep project files and project notes all in one place.

Simply drag and drop any file from Microsoft Windows Explorer onto a page in Microsoft OneNote, or insert them by using **Insert, Files** on the OneNote menu.

You can open and edit an attached file by double-clicking its file icon.

I hope all these Windows 7 and Office 2010 tips have been useful and you will practice them until they become second nature to you. With the time you save, you can take on new challenges at work that tap into your own passion to help you and your company.

Extras

These are some of the extra programs which I personally found very useful. They are included with the intention of driving awareness to some of the free tools and hidden features of common programs which may benefit some of the users.

A. Windows Live Mail®

I was a regular user of Outlook at work and Yahoo e-mail for personal use. I never had a reason to switch e-mail providers. I had accounts at Hotmail, Excite, Gmail and various other providers where I could check out the features from time to time, but Yahoo was enough for my own use.

Then everything changed. With Live.com, I had an opportunity to create a new ID, so I created a Windows Live ID and downloaded the Windows Live mail client. It was the best decision I ever made. Now I get the same seamless experience of a rich client e-mail with the assurance of Web access if I ever need to log-in from a kiosk or another PC. However the best part was it imported 10 years' worth of e-mail from Yahoo In no time.

Go to http://explore.live.com/windows-live-mail and download the Windows Live Essentials, which includes free programs for photos, movies, instant messaging, e-mail, blogging, family safety, and more.

You can get Calendar, Events, Shared Calendars and aggregate e-mails on one client for online and offline access. It is very cool!

B. Internet Explorer® InPrivate Browsing

Have you ever been uncomfortable in checking your e-mail from a public computer? Or were hesitant to use online banking, for the fear of someone accessing your account info? The InPrivate browsing of Internet Explorer is the way to go.

Step 1 – Launch Internet Explorer 8.

- o For Internet Explorer 9 Go to Settings and navigate to tools.

Step 2 – Go to InPrivate Browsing

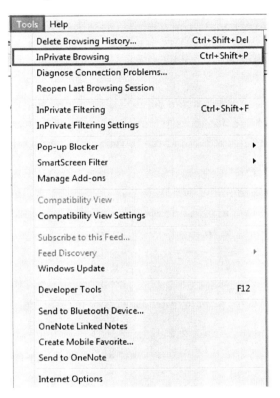

Figure 233

This launches as a private session. InPrivate browsing helps prevent Microsoft Internet Explorer from storing data about your browsing session. This includes cookies, temporary Internet files, history and other data. Toolbars and extensions are also disabled by default.

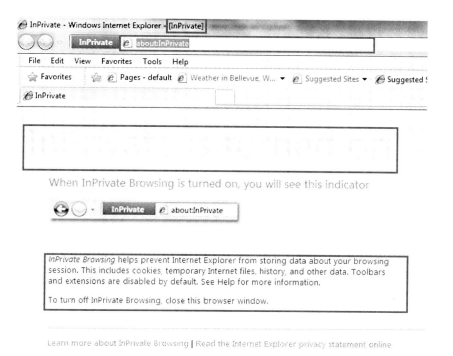

When InPrivate Browsing is turned on, you will see this indicator

InPrivate Browsing helps prevent Internet Explorer from storing data about your browsing session. This includes cookies, temporary Internet files, history, and other data. Toolbars and extensions are disabled by default. See Help for more information.

To turn off InPrivate Browsing, close this browser window.

Learn more about InPrivate Browsing | Read the Internet Explorer privacy statement online

Figure 234

To quickly get to an InPrivate view just type in **CTRL+SHIFT+P**.

C. Internet Explorer® Tab sorter

This works in Internet Explorer 8

Click on Quick Tabs – CTRL+Q to quickly toggle between all the active tabs of Internet Explorer and select any tab you want to go to. I find it very handy when I have several tabs open at the same time.

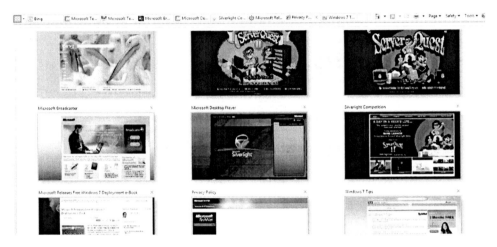

Figure 235

D. Windows Live SkyDrive®

Figure 236

This one the best-kept secrets which is available for anyone to use. And it's **free!**

SkyDrive gives an amazing 25GB of free online "cloud" storage. That's approximately 8,000 photos, or around 5,000 MP3s. Here are some of the key features:

- You control who can see your files online.
- You can set a folder to private and you can access it from any PC connected to the internet. This makes it ideal for backing up files online.
- You can set a folder's permissions to "public" or share it with individuals, meaning that you can securely share files with colleagues, friends, or family.

Authors note: This entire book was written using SkyDrive, to share the files with the editors, designers, reviewers etc.

Drag, drop and upload

Uploading your files to SkyDrive is very easy: simply drag your files from your computer and drop them into SkyDrive. You can then create multiple folders, set permissions and send an invitation to your friends or co-workers. Each file on SkyDrive has a unique URL that you can easily share with your contacts, making online file sharing simple.

You can access it at http://skydrive.live.com

E. Blocking Sites to Get More Productivity

If you are looking for gains in productivity, then follow this simple step. I am sure you will end up with countless extra minutes (or hours) in the day. Admit it, we each have our favorites:

- Social Networking sites
- Sports sites
- Auction/collector sites
- Video sites, or in the case of my kids, cartoon sites
- or, in my case, web sites on cricket statistics

To avoid being distracted, follow these simple steps

Step 1 - Launch Microsoft Internet Explorer
Step 2 – Go to Tools

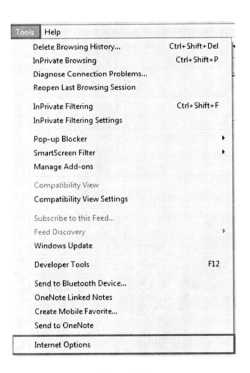

Figure 237

Step 3 – Select **Security, Restricted sites, Sites**

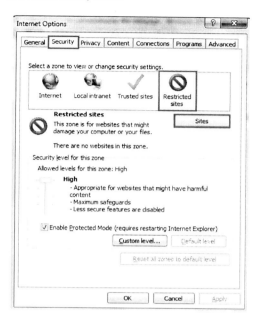

Figure 238

Enter the sites you want to block or could hinder your work productivity. (Note: the sites listed are only for example purposes and do not reflect the author's views or recommendations.)

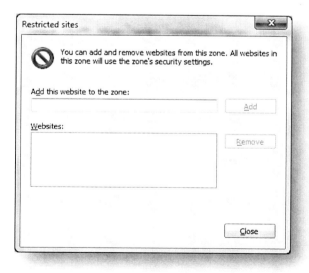

Figure 239

Here is what my selection looks like -- or at least when I am at work. ☺

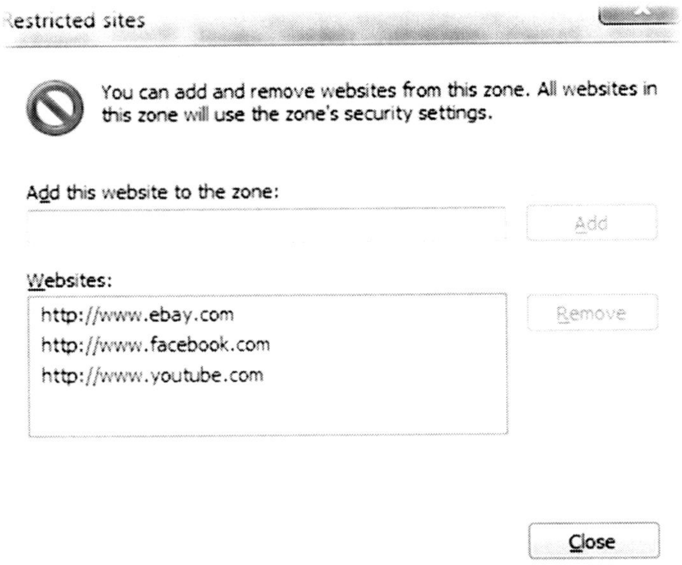

Restricted sites

You can add and remove websites from this zone. All websites in
this zone will use the zone's security settings.

Add this website to the zone:

[   ]   Add

Websites:

http://www.ebay.com   Remove
http://www.facebook.com
http://www.youtube.com

Close

Figure 240

Cheat Sheets

Microsoft Windows® 7

Task	Quick Key
Connect to a projector - Windows + P	Windows logo key +P
Lock your machine	Windows logo key +L
Access the Mobility Center	Windows logo key +X
Show Desktop	Windows logo key +D
Quick Search	Windows logo key +F.
Split Window- Windows Snap	Windows logo key +Left Arrow Windows logo key +Right Arrow
Open the Run dialog box.	Windows logo key +R
Minimize all windows.	Windows logo key +M
Restore minimized windows to the desktop.	Windows logo key +Shift+M
Open Computer.	Windows logo key +E
Cycle through programs on the taskbar.	Windows logo key +T
Start the program pinned to the taskbar in the position indicated by the number. If the program is already running, switch to that program.	Windows logo key +*number*
Start a new instance of the program pinned to the taskbar in the position indicated by the number.	Shift+Windows logo key +*number*
Switch to the last active window of the program pinned to the taskbar in the position indicated by the number.	Ctrl+Windows logo key +*number*
Open the Jump List for the program pinned to the taskbar in the position indicated by the number.	Alt + Windows logo key +*number*
Cycle through programs on the taskbar by using Aero Flip 3-D.	Windows logo key +Tab
Use the arrow keys to cycle through programs on the taskbar by using Aero Flip 3-D.	Ctrl + Windows logo key +Tab
Preview the desktop.	Windows logo key +Spacebar
Maximize the window.	Windows logo key +Up Arrow
Minimize the window.	Windows logo key +Down Arrow

Minimize all but the active window.	Windows logo key ⊞+Home
Stretch the window to the top and bottom of the screen.	Windows logo key ⊞+ Shift + Up Arrow
Minimize all but the active window.	Windows logo key ⊞+D
Stretch the window to the top and bottom of the screen.	Windows logo key ⊞+Left Arrow
© www.vyanjan.com	

Microsoft Outlook®2010

Task	Quick Key
New e-mail message	CTRL+N
Send an e-mail message	CTRL + Enter
Send and Receive mail	CTRL+M
Delete an E-mail	CTRL+D
Open the Address Book	CTRL+Shift+B
Forward a message	CTRL+F
Go to Next unread message	CTRL+U
Go to Folder	CTRL+Y
Open Selected message	CTRL+O
Check Spelling	F7
Insert signature	CTRL+SHIFT+S
Send (post) a message	CTRL+ENTER or ALT+S
New meeting request	CTRL + SHIFT +Q
Create a bulleted list	CTRL + SHIFT + L
© www.vyanjan.com	

Microsoft Excel®2010

Task	Quick Key
New e-mail message	CTRL+N
New file	Ctrl + N
Open file	Ctrl + O
Save file	Ctrl + S
Move between open workbooks	Ctrl + F6
Close file	Ctrl + F4
Save as	F12
Display the print menu	Ctrl + P
Select whole spreadsheet	Ctrl + A
Select column	Ctrl + Space
Select row	Shift + Space
Undo last action	Ctrl + Z
Redo last action	Ctrl + Y
Start a formula	Equals Sign (e.g. SUM(A1+A2)
New file	Ctrl + N
Open file	Ctrl + O
Save file	Ctrl + S
Move between open workbooks	Ctrl + F6
Close file	Ctrl + F4
Save as	F12
Display the print menu	Ctrl + P
Select whole spreadsheet	Ctrl + A
Select column	Ctrl + Space
© www.vyanjan.com	

Microsoft Word®2010

Task	Quick Key
CTRL and A.	Selects all in the current document
CTRL and B	Bold text.
CTRL and C	Copies the item or text to the Clipboard and can be pasted using CTRL and V.
CTRL and D	Displays the Font dialogue box.
CTRL and E	Centre Alignment.
CTRL and F	Displays the Find dialog box, to search the current document.
CTRL and G	Displays the Go to dialog box, to go to a specific location in the current document.
CTRL and H	Displays the Replace dialogue box.
CTRL and I	Italic text.
CTRL and J	Full Justification.
CTRL and K	Create Hyperlink
CTRL and L	Left Alignment
CTRL and M	Tab
CTRL and N	Creates a new document.
CTRL and O	Displays the Open File dialogue box.
CTRL and P	Displays the Print dialog box.
CTRL and R	Right Alignment.
CTRL and S	Displays the Save dialog box.
© www.vyanjan.com	

151

Microsoft OneNote® 2010

Task	Quick Key
Open a new OneNote window.	CTRL+M
Open a small OneNote window to create a side note.	CTRL+SHIFT+M
Undo the last action.	CTRL+Z
Redo the last action.	CTRL+Y
Select all items.	CTRL+A
Cut the selected text or item.	CTRL+X
Copy the selected text or item to the Clipboard.	CTRL+C
Paste the contents of the Clipboard.	CTRL+V
Move to the beginning of the line.	HOME
Turn overtype mode on or off.	INSERT
Move to the end of the line.	END
Move one character to the left.	LEFT ARROW
Move one character to the right.	RIGHT ARROW
Move one word to the left.	CTRL+LEFT ARROW
Move one word to the right.	CTRL+RIGHT ARROW
Delete one character to the left.	BACKSPACE
Delete one character to the right.	DELETE
Delete one word to the left.	CTRL+BACKSPACE
Delete one word to the right.	CTRL+DELETE
Insert a line break.	SHIFT+ENTER
© www.vyanjan.com	

Appendix

The Windows Graphical User Interface

The diagram below shows the elements and standard terminology of the Windows Graphical User Interface.

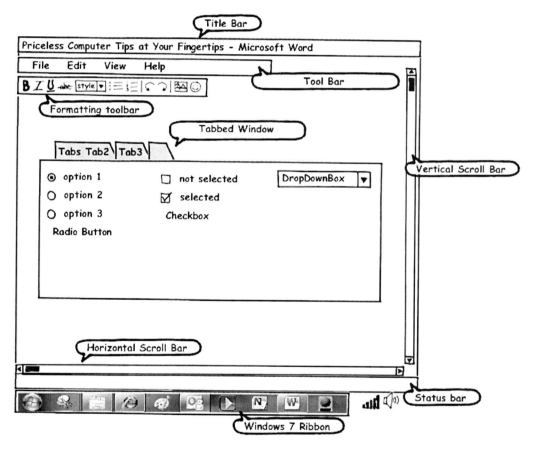

Figure 241

What is a Right Click on a mouse?

Most Windows applications use the mouse's Right Click to activate very helpful, commonly used sub-menus or commands. The diagram below indicates the Right Click on a mouse.

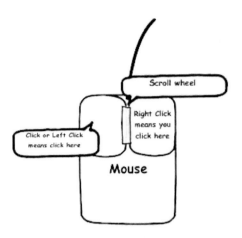

Figure 242

Useful Sites

These links are provided for your convenience. The author has no responsibility for the content of the linked website(s).

Microsoft Office Site http://office.microsoft.com/en-us/
Lots of free templates, background designs and tips on using the various Microsoft Office Products

Microsoft Windows Site http://windows.microsoft.com/en-US/windows/home
Your definitive guide to Windows resources, Help and How to tips on most topics.

Microsoft Most Valuable Professional (MVP) Blog sites - http://www.mvps.org/links.html
A treasury of sites and links to possibly the most dedicated and selfless army of experts on various Microsoft products serving the community. Definitely it is my favorite site.

How to Geek http://www.howtogeek.com/
This gem of a site covers a broad range of technology tips from a wide variety of topics such as Operating Systems, Networking, Phones, etc. A must-read for new ideas.

Microsoft TechNet www.technet.com for IT Professionals.
Microsoft MSDN www.msdn.com for Developers.

Lifehacker – A very good site that helps you save time, work smarter and get the most out of technology, with productivity tips, downloads, shortcuts and website recommendations. www.lifehacker.com.

Book Ordering

If you would like to order more copies of this book please visit www.vyanjan.com or send an email to book@vyanjan.com

CPSIA information can be obtained at www.ICGtesting.com
Printed in the USA
LVOW031817140912

298879LV00005B/32/P